chocolate
heaven

chocolate *heaven*

irresistible recipes to die for

christine france

HERMES
HOUSE

This edition is published by Hermes House

Hermes House is an imprint of Anness Publishing Ltd
Hermes House, 88–89 Blackfriars Road, London SE1 8HA
tel. 020 7401 2077; fax 020 7633 9499; info@anness.com

Published in the USA by Hermes House, Anness Publishing Inc.
27 West 20th Street, New York, NY 10011; fax 212 807 6813

Publisher: Joanna Lorenz
Project Editors: Joanne Rippin, Linda Doeser
Assistant Editor: Emma Gray
Designers: Nigel Partridge, Siân Keogh
Special Photography: Don Last
Cover Design: Axis Design Editions Ltd

Previously published as *Chocolate Fantasies*

10 9 8 7 6 5 4 3 2 1

The authors and publishers would like to thank the following people for
supplying additional recipes in the book: Catherine Atkinson, Alex Barker,
Carla Capalbo, Maxine Clark, Frances Cleary, Carole Clements, Roz Denny,
Nicola Diggins, Joanne Farrow, Silvana Franco, Sarah Gates, Shirley Gill,
Patricia Lousada, Norma MacMillan, Sue Maggs, Sarah Maxwell, Janice
Murfitt, Annie Nichols, Angela Nilsen, Louise Pickford, Katherine
Richmond, Hilaire Walden, Laura Washburn, Steven Wheeler, Judy Williams,
Elizabeth Wolf-Cohen.

Additional recipe photographs supplied by: Karl Adamson, Edward
Allwright, David Armstrong, Steve Baxter, James Duncan, Michelle Garrett,
Amanda Heywood, Tim Hill, David Jordan.

NOTES
For all recipes, quantities are given in both metric and imperial measures and,
where appropriate, measures are given in standard cups and spoons.
Follow one set, but not a mixture, because they are not interchangeable.

Standard spoon and cup measurements are level.
1 tsp = 5ml, 1 tbsp = 15ml; 1 cup = 250ml/8fl oz

Australian standard tablespoons are 20ml. Australian readers should use 3
tsp in place of 1 tbsp for measuring small quantities of gelatine, cornflour,
salt etc.

Medium eggs should be used unless otherwise stated.

 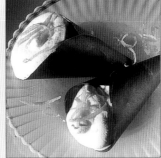 

CONTENTS

INTRODUCTION	6
CAKES & GATEAUX	12
HOT DESSERTS	32
TARTS, PIES & CHEESECAKES	42
COLD DESSERTS	58
LITTLE CAKES, BISCUITS & BARS	74
SWEETS & TRUFFLES	86
INDEX	96

INTRODUCTION

Few people can resist it – whether a sumptuous and self-indulgent chocolate gâteau, a plate of melt-in-the-mouth profiteroles, a richly coated sundae or a decorative box of truffles. This book is packed with wickedly tempting recipes for those with a sweet tooth, chocolate-lovers and self-admitted, outright "chocoholics".

The book is divided into six chapters, with over 70 recipes for preparing superb confections with dark, milk and white chocolate. Cakes & Gâteaux ranges from morning coffee and afternoon tea-time treats, such as Chocolate Coconut Roulade and Frosted Chocolate Fudge, to magnificent dinner party centrepieces, such as Chocolate Redcurrant Torte and Meringue Gâteau with Chocolate Mascarpone. Hot Desserts includes such magical delights as Chocolate Crêpes with Plums and Port and Dark Chocolate Ravioli with White Chocolate and Cream Cheese Filling. Tarts, Pies & Cheesecakes boasts such favourites as Chocolate Tiramisu Tart and Mississippi Mud Pie, while Cold Desserts tantalizes the tastebuds with a selection of sorbets and ice creams. Anything from Little Cakes, Biscuits & Bars will bring the children running, while Sweets & Truffles offers more sophisticated pleasures, such as Double Chocolate-dipped Fruit, Rich Chocolate Pistachio Fudge and Cognac and Ginger Creams.

There is hardly a country in the western world that does not have chocolate as part of its culinary culture, whether it be a moist chocolate brownie from the United States, a chocolate-covered pancake from Hungary or an elegant French pastry. Indulge yourself on a chocolate-lover's dream journey – your only problem will be what to choose next!

TECHNIQUES

MELTING CHOCOLATE

If chocolate is being melted on its own, all the equipment must be completely dry, as water may cause the chocolate to thicken and become a stiff paste. For this reason, do not cover chocolate during or after melting it, as condensation could form. If chocolate does thicken, add a little pure white vegetable fat (not butter or margarine) and mix well. If this does not work, start again. Do not discard the thickened chocolate; melt it with cream to make a sauce.

With or without liquid, chocolate should be melted very slowly. It is easily burned or scorched, and then develops a bad flavour. If any steam gets into the chocolate, it can turn into a solid mass. If this happens, stir in a little pure white vegetable fat. Dark chocolate should not be heated above 50°C/120°F. Milk and white chocolate should not be heated above 45°C/110°F. Take particular care when melting white chocolate, which clogs very easily when subjected to heat.

MELTING CHOCOLATE OVER SIMMERING WATER

<u>1</u> Chop or cut the chocolate into small pieces with a sharp knife to enable it to melt quickly and evenly.

<u>2</u> Put the chocolate in the top of a double boiler or in a heatproof bowl over a saucepan of barely simmering water. The bowl should not touch the water.

<u>3</u> Heat gently until the chocolate is melted and smooth, stirring occasionally. Remove from the heat and stir.

MELTING CHOCOLATE OVER DIRECT HEAT

When a recipe recommends melting chocolate with a liquid such as milk, cream or even butter, this can be done over direct heat in a saucepan.

<u>1</u> Choose a heavy-based saucepan. Add the chocolate and liquid and melt over a low heat, stirring frequently, until the chocolate is melted and the mixture is smooth. Remove from heat immediately. This method is also used for making sauces, icings and some sweets.

<u>2</u> Chocolate can also be melted in a very low oven. Preheat oven to 110°C/225°F/Gas ¼. Put the chocolate in an ovenproof bowl and place in the oven for a few minutes. Remove the chocolate before it is completely melted and stir until smooth.

MELTING CHOCOLATE IN THE MICROWAVE

Check the chocolate at frequent intervals during the cooking time. These times are for a 650–700 W oven and are approximate, as microwave ovens vary.

<u>1</u> Place 115g/4oz chopped or broken dark, bittersweet or semi-sweet chocolate in a microwave-safe bowl and microwave on Medium for about 2 minutes. The same quantity of milk or white chocolate should be melted on Low for about 2 minutes.

<u>2</u> Check the chocolate frequently during the cooking time. The chocolate will not change shape, but will start to look shiny. It must then be removed from the microwave and stirred until completely melted and smooth.

TEMPERING CHOCOLATE

TEMPERING CHOCOLATE

Tempering is the process of gently heating and cooling chocolate to stabilize the emulsification of cocoa solids and butterfat. This technique is generally used by professionals handling couverture chocolate. It allows the chocolate to shrink quickly (to allow easy release from a mould, for example with Easter eggs) or to be kept at room temperature for several weeks or months without losing its crispness and shiny surface. All solid chocolate is tempered in production, but once melted loses its "temper" and must be tempered again unless it is to be used immediately. Untempered chocolate tends to "bloom" or becomes dull and streaky or takes on a cloudy appearance. This can be avoided if the melted chocolate is put in the fridge immediately: chilling the chocolate solidifies the cocoa butter and prevents it from rising to the surface and "blooming". General baking and dessert-making do not require tempering, which is a fussy procedure and takes practice. However, it is useful to be aware of the technique when preparing sophisticated decorations, moulded chocolates or coatings. Most shapes can be made without tempering if they are chilled immediately.

EQUIPMENT

To temper chocolate successfully, you will need a marble slab or similar cool, smooth surface, such as an upturned baking sheet. A flexible plastic scraper is ideal for spreading the chocolate, but you can use a palette knife. As the temperature is crucial, you will need a chocolate thermometer. Look for this at a specialist kitchen supply shop, where you may also find blocks of tempered chocolate, ready for immediate use.

1 Break up the chocolate into small pieces and place it in the top of a double boiler or a heatproof bowl over a saucepan of hot water. Heat gently until just melted.

2 Remove from the heat. Spoon about three-quarters of the melted chocolate on to a marble slab or other cool, smooth, non-porous work surface.

3 With a flexible plastic scraper or palette knife, spread the chocolate thinly, then scoop it up before spreading it again. Repeat the sequence, keeping the chocolate constantly on the move, for about 5 minutes.

4 Using a chocolate thermometer, check the temperature of the chocolate as you work it. As soon as the temperature registers 28°C/82°F, tip the chocolate back into the bowl and stir into the remaining chocolate.

5 With the addition of the hot chocolate, the temperature should now be 32°C/90°F, making the chocolate ready for use. To test, drop a little of the chocolate from a spoon on to the marble; it should set very quickly.

STORING CHOCOLATE

Chocolate can be stored successfully for up to a year if the conditions are favourable. This means a dry place with a temperature of around 20°C/68°F. At higher temperatures, the chocolate may develop white streaks as the fat comes to the surface. Although this will not spoil the flavour, it will mar the appearance of the chocolate, making it unsuitable for use as a decoration. When storing chocolate, keep it cool and dry. Place inside an airtight container, away from strong smelling foods. Check the "best before" dates on the pack.

Piping with Chocolate

Pipe chocolate directly on to a cake, or on to non-stick baking paper to make run-outs, small outlined shapes or irregular designs. After melting the chocolate, allow it to cool slightly so it just coats the back of a spoon. If it still flows freely it will be too runny to hold its shape when piped. When it is the right consistency, you then need to work fast as the chocolate will set quickly. Use a paper piping bag and keep the pressure very tight, as the chocolate will flow readily without encouragement.

Making a Paper Piping Bag

A non-stick paper cone is ideal for piping small amounts of messy liquids like chocolate as it is small, easy to handle and disposable, unlike a conventional piping bag, which will need cleaning.

1 Fold a square of non-stick baking paper in half to form a triangle. With the triangle point facing you, fold the left corner down to the centre.

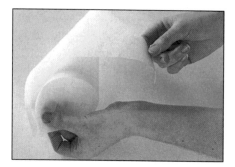

2 Fold the right corner down and wrap it around the folded left corner to form a cone. Fold the ends into the cone.

3 Spoon the melted chocolate into the cone and fold the top edges over. When ready to pipe, snip off the end of the point neatly to make a tiny hole, about 3 mm / ⅛ in in diameter.

4 Another method is to use a small heavy-duty freezer or plastic bag. Place a piping nozzle in one corner of the bag, so that it is in the correct position for piping. Fill as above, squeezing the filling into one corner and twisting the top to seal. Snip off the corner of the bag, if necessary, so that the tip of the nozzle emerges, and squeeze gently to pipe the design.

Chocolate Drizzles

You can have great fun making random shapes or, with a steady hand, special designs that will look great on cakes or biscuits.

1 Melt the chocolate and pour it into a paper cone or small piping bag fitted with a very small plain nozzle. Drizzle the chocolate on to a baking sheet lined with non-stick baking paper to make small, self-contained lattice shapes, such as circles or squares. Allow to set for 30 minutes then peel off the paper.

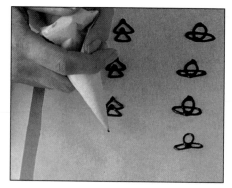

2 Chocolate can be used in many designs, such as flowers or butterflies. Use non-stick baking paper as tracing paper and pipe the chocolate over the chosen design or decorative shape.

3 For butterflies, pipe chocolate on to individually cut squares and leave until just beginning to set. Use a long, thin box (such as an egg carton) and place the butterfly shape in the box or between the cups so it is bent in the centre, creating the butterfly shape. Chill until needed.

Piping on to Cakes

This looks effective on top of a cake iced with coffee glacé icing.

1 Melt 50g/2oz each of white and plain dark chocolate in separate bowls, and allow to cool slightly. Place the chocolates in separate paper piping bags. Cut a small piece off the pointed end of each bag in a straight line.

2 Hold each piping bag in turn above the surface of the cake and pipe the chocolates all over as shown in the picture. Alternatively, pipe a freehand design in one continuous curvy line, first with one bag of chocolate, then the other.

PIPING CURLS

Make lots of these curly shapes and store them in a cool place ready for using as cake decorations. Try piping the lines in contrasting colours of chocolate to vary the effect.

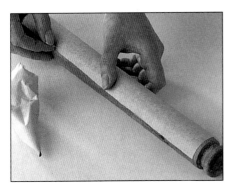

1 Melt 115g/4oz chocolate and allow to cool slightly. Cover a rolling pin with baking parchment and attach it with tape. Fill a paper piping bag with the chocolate and cut a small piece off the pointed end in a straight line.

2 Pipe lines of chocolate backwards and forwards over the baking parchment.

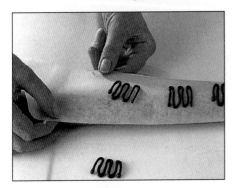

3 Leave the piped curls to set in a cool place, then carefully peel off the baking parchment. Use a palette knife to lift the curls on to the cake.

FEATHERING OR MARBLING CHOCOLATE

These two related techniques provide some of the easiest and most effective ways of decorating the top of a cake, and they are also used when making a swirled mixture for cut-outs. Chocolate sauce and double cream can also be feathered or marbled to decorate a dessert.

1 Melt two contrasting colours of chocolate and spread one over the cake or surface to be decorated.

2 Spoon the contrasting chocolate into a piping bag and pipe lines or swirls over the chocolate base.

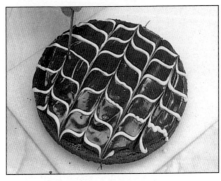

3 Working quickly before the chocolate sets, draw a skewer or cocktail stick through the swirls to create a feathered or marbled effect.

CHOCOLATE RUN-OUTS

Try piping the outline in one colour of chocolate and filling in the middle with another. The effect can be dramatic.

1 Tape a piece of greaseproof paper to a baking sheet or flat board. Draw around a shaped biscuit cutter on to the paper several times. Secure a piece of non-stick baking paper over the top.

2 Pipe over the outline of your design in a continuous thread.

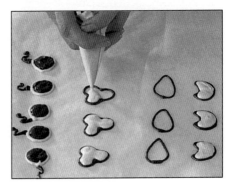

3 Cut the end off the other bag, making the hole slightly wider than before, and pipe the chocolate to fill in the outline so it looks slightly rounded. Leave the shapes to set in a cool place, then carefully lift them off the non-stick baking paper with a palette knife.

CAKES &
GATEAUX

FRENCH CHOCOLATE CAKE

SERVES 10

250g / 9oz bittersweet chocolate, chopped into small pieces
225g / 8oz / 1 cup unsalted butter, cut into small pieces
90g / 3½oz / scant ½ cup granulated sugar
30ml / 2 tbsp brandy or orange-flavoured liqueur
5 eggs
15ml / 1 tbsp plain flour
icing sugar, for dusting
whipped or soured cream, for serving

1 Preheat oven to 180°C / 350°F / Gas 4. Generously grease a 23 x 5 cm / 9 x 2 in springform tin. Line the base with non-stick baking paper and grease. Wrap the bottom and sides of the tin in foil to prevent water from seeping through into the cake.

2 In a saucepan, over a low heat, melt the chocolate, butter and sugar, stirring frequently until smooth. Remove from the heat, cool slightly and stir in the brandy or liqueur.

3 In a large bowl beat the eggs lightly for 1 minute. Beat in the flour, then slowly beat in the chocolate mixture until well blended. Pour into the tin.

4 Place the springform tin in a large roasting tin. Add enough boiling water to come 2 cm / ¾ in up the side of the springform tin. Bake for 25–30 minutes, until the edge of the cake is set but the centre is still soft. Remove the springform tin from the roasting tin and remove the foil. Cool on a wire rack. The cake will sink in the centre and become its classic slim shape as it cools. Don't worry if the surface cracks slightly.

5 Remove the side of the springform tin and turn the cake on to a wire rack. Lift off the springform tin base and then carefully peel back the paper, so the base of the cake is now the top. Leave the cake on the rack until it is quite cold.

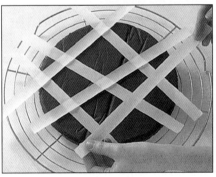

6 Cut 6–8 strips of non-stick baking paper 2.5 cm / 1 in wide and place randomly over the cake. Dust the cake with icing sugar, then carefully remove the paper. Slide the cake on to a plate and serve with whipped or soured cream.

MERINGUE GATEAU WITH CHOCOLATE MASCARPONE

SERVES ABOUT 10

4 egg whites
pinch of salt
175g/6oz/¾ cup caster sugar
5ml/1 tsp ground cinnamon
75g/3oz plain dark chocolate, grated
icing sugar and rose petals, to decorate

FOR THE FILLING

115g/4oz plain chocolate, chopped into
small pieces
5ml/1 tsp vanilla essence or rosewater
115g/4oz/½ cup mascarpone cheese

1 Preheat oven to 150°C/300°F/Gas 2. Line two large baking sheets with non-stick baking paper. Whisk the egg whites with the salt in a clean, grease-free bowl until they form stiff peaks.
2 Gradually whisk in half the sugar, then add the rest and whisk until the meringue is very stiff and glossy. Add the cinnamon and chocolate and whisk lightly to mix.

3 Draw a 20 cm/8 in circle on the lining paper on one of the baking sheets, replace it upside down and spread the marked circle evenly with about half the meringue. Spoon the remaining meringue in 28–30 small neat heaps on both baking sheets. Bake for 1½ hours, until crisp.

4 Make the filling. Melt the chocolate in a heatproof bowl over hot water. Cool slightly, then add the vanilla essence or rosewater and cheese. Cool the mixture until it holds it shape.

5 Spoon the chocolate mixture into a large piping bag and sandwich the meringues together in pairs, reserving a small amount of filling for assembling the gâteau.
6 Arrange the filled meringues on a serving platter, piling them up in a pyramid. Keep them in position with a few well-placed dabs of the reserved filling. Dust the pyramid with icing sugar, sprinkle with the rose petals and serve at once, while the meringues are crisp.

CHOCOLATE ALMOND MOUSSE CAKE

SERVES 8

*50g/2oz plain dark chocolate, broken
into squares*
200g/7oz marzipan, grated or chopped
200ml/7fl oz/scant 1 cup milk
115g/4oz/1 cup self-raising flour
2 eggs, separated
*75g/3oz/½ cup light muscovado
sugar*

FOR THE MOUSSE FILLING

*115g/4oz plain chocolate, chopped into
small pieces*
50g/2oz/¼ cup unsalted butter
2 eggs, separated
*30ml/2 tbsp Amaretto di Saronno
liqueur*

FOR THE TOPPING

1 quantity Chocolate Ganache
toasted flaked almonds, to decorate

1 Preheat oven to 190°C/375°F/Gas 5. Grease a deep 17 cm/6½ in square cake tin and line with non-stick baking paper. Combine the chocolate, marzipan and milk in a saucepan and heat gently without boiling, stirring until smooth.

2 Sift the flour into a bowl and add the chocolate mixture and egg yolks, beating until evenly mixed.

3 Whisk the egg whites in a clean, grease-free bowl until stiff enough to hold firm peaks. Whisk in the sugar gradually. Stir about 15ml/1 tbsp of the whites into the chocolate mixture to lighten it, then fold in the rest.

4 Spoon the mixture into the tin, spreading it evenly. Bake for 45–50 minutes, until well risen, firm and springy to the touch. Leave to cool on a wire rack.

5 Make the mousse filling. Melt the chocolate with the butter in a small saucepan over a low heat, then remove from the heat and beat in the egg yolks and Amaretto. Whisk the egg whites in a clean, grease-free bowl until stiff, then fold into the chocolate mixture.

6 Slice the cold cake in half across the middle to make two even layers. Return one half to the clean cake tin and pour over the chocolate mousse. Top with the second layer of cake and press down lightly. Chill until set.

7 Turn the cake out on to a serving plate. Allow the chocolate ganache to soften to room temperature, then beat it to a soft, spreading consistency. Spread the chocolate ganache over the top and sides of the cake, then press toasted flaked almonds over the sides. Serve chilled.

SACHERTORTE

SERVES 10–12

*225g/8oz plain dark chocolate, chopped into
small pieces*
150g/5oz/⅔ cup butter, softened
115g/4oz/½ cup caster sugar
8 eggs, separated
115g/4oz/1 cup plain flour
FOR THE GLAZE
225g/8oz/scant 1 cup apricot jam
15ml/1 tbsp lemon juice
FOR THE ICING
*225g/8oz plain dark chocolate, cut into
small pieces*
200g/7oz/scant 1 cup caster sugar
15ml/1 tbsp golden syrup
250ml/8fl oz/1 cup double cream
5ml/1 tsp vanilla essence
plain chocolate leaves, to decorate

1 Preheat oven to 180°C/350°F/Gas 4.
Grease a 23 cm/9 in round springform
cake tin and line with non-stick baking
paper. Melt the chocolate in a heatproof
bowl over barely simmering water, then
set the bowl aside.

2 Cream the butter with the sugar in a
mixing bowl until pale and fluffy, then
add the egg yolks, one at a time, beating
after each addition. Beat in the melted
chocolate, then sift the flour over the
mixture and fold it in evenly.

3 Whisk the egg whites in a clean, grease-
free bowl until stiff, then stir about a
quarter of the whites into the chocolate
mixture to lighten it. Fold in the
remaining whites.

4 Tip the chocolate mixture into the
prepared cake tin and smooth level. Bake
for about 50–55 minutes or until firm.
Cool in the tin for 5 minutes, then turn
out carefully on to a wire rack and leave
to cool completely.

5 Make the glaze. Heat the apricot jam
with the lemon juice in a small saucepan
until melted, then strain through a sieve
into a bowl. Once the cake is cold, slice
in half across the middle to make two
even-size layers.

6 Brush the top and sides of each layer
with the apricot glaze, then sandwich
them together. Place on a wire rack.

7 Make the icing. Mix the chocolate,
sugar, golden syrup, cream and vanilla
essence in a heavy saucepan. Heat gently,
stirring constantly, until the mixture is
thick and smooth. Simmer gently for 3–5
minutes, without stirring, until the
mixture registers 95°C/200°F on a sugar
thermometer. Pour the icing quickly over
the cake, spreading to cover the top and
sides completely. Leave to set, decorate
with chocolate leaves, then serve with
whipped cream, if wished.

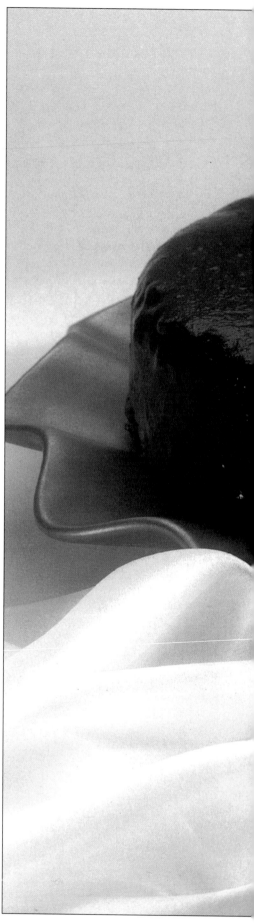

BLACK FOREST GATEAU

4 Prick each layer all over with a skewer or fork, then sprinkle with Kirsch. Using a hand-held electric mixer, whip the cream in a bowl until it starts to thicken, then gradually beat in the icing sugar and vanilla essence until the mixture begins to hold its shape.

5 To assemble, spread one cake layer with a thick layer of flavoured cream and top with about half the cherries. Spread a second cake layer with cream, top with the remaining cherries, then place it on top of the first layer. Top with the final cake layer.

6 Spread the remaining cream all over the cake. Dust a plate with icing sugar, and position the cake carefully in the centre. Press grated chocolate over the sides and decorate the cake with the chocolate curls and fresh or drained cherries.

SERVES 8–10
6 eggs
200g/7oz/scant 1 cup caster sugar
5ml/1 tsp vanilla essence
50g/2oz/½ cup plain flour
50g/2oz/½ cup cocoa powder
115g/4oz/½ cup unsalted butter, melted
FOR THE FILLING AND TOPPING
60ml/4 tbsp Kirsch
600ml/1 pint/2½ cups double cream
30ml/2 tbsp icing sugar
2.5ml/½ tsp vanilla essence
675g/1½lb jar stoned morello cherries,
well drained
TO DECORATE
icing sugar, for dusting
grated chocolate
Chocolate Curls
fresh or drained canned morello cherries

1 Preheat oven to 180°C/350°F/Gas 4. Grease three 19 cm/7½ in sandwich cake tins. Line the bottom of each with non-stick baking paper. Combine the eggs with the sugar and vanilla essence in a bowl and beat with a hand-held electric mixer until pale and very thick.
2 Sift the flour and cocoa powder over the mixture and fold in lightly and evenly with a metal spoon. Gently stir in the melted butter.
3 Divide the mixture among the prepared cake tins, smoothing them level. Bake for 15–18 minutes, until the cakes have risen and are springy to the touch. Leave them to cool in the tins for about 5 minutes, then turn out on to wire racks and leave to cool completely. Remove the lining paper from each cake layer.

CHOCOLATE GINGER CRUNCH CAKE

SERVES 6

150g/5oz plain chocolate, chopped into small pieces
50g/2oz/¼ cup unsalted butter
115g/4oz ginger nut biscuits
4 pieces of preserved stem ginger
30ml/2 tbsp stem ginger syrup
45ml/3 tbsp desiccated coconut

TO DECORATE

25g/1oz milk chocolate, chopped into small pieces
pieces of crystallized ginger

1 Grease a 15 cm/6 in flan ring and place it on a sheet of non-stick baking paper. Melt the plain chocolate with the butter in a heatproof bowl over barely simmering water. Remove from the heat and set aside.

2 Crush the biscuits into small pieces. Tip them into a bowl.

3 Chop the stem ginger fairly finely and mix with the crushed ginger nut biscuits.

4 Stir the biscuit mixture, ginger syrup and coconut into the melted chocolate and butter, mixing well until evenly combined.

5 Tip the mixture into the prepared flan ring and press down firmly and evenly. Chill in the fridge until set.

6 Remove the flan ring and slide the cake on to a plate. Melt the milk chocolate, drizzle it over the top and decorate with the pieces of crystallized ginger.

FROSTED CHOCOLATE FUDGE CAKE

SERVES 6–8

115g/4oz plain chocolate, chopped into small pieces
175g/6oz/¾ cup unsalted butter or margarine, softened
200g/7oz/generous 1 cup light muscovado sugar
5ml/1 tsp vanilla essence
3 eggs, beaten
150ml/¼ pint/⅔ cup Greek-style yogurt
150g/5oz/1¼ cups self-raising flour
icing sugar and chocolate curls, to decorate

FOR THE FROSTING

115g/4 oz plain dark chocolate, chopped into small pieces
50g/2oz/¼ cup unsalted butter
350g/12oz/2¼ cups icing sugar
90ml/6 tbsp Greek-style yogurt

1 Preheat oven to 190°C/375°F/Gas 5. Lightly grease two 20 cm/8 in round sandwich cake tins and line the base of each with non-stick baking paper. Melt the chocolate.

2 In a mixing bowl, cream the butter or margarine with the sugar until light and fluffy. Beat in the vanilla essence, then gradually add the beaten eggs, beating well after each addition.

3 Stir in the melted plain chocolate and yogurt evenly. Fold in the flour with a metal spoon.

4 Divide the mixture between the prepared tins. Bake for 25–30 minutes or until the cakes are firm to the touch. Turn out and cool on a wire rack.

5 Make the frosting. Melt the chocolate and butter in a saucepan over a low heat. Remove from the heat and stir in the icing sugar and yogurt. Mix with a rubber spatula until smooth, then beat until the frosting begins to cool and thicken slightly. Use about a third of the mixture to sandwich the cakes together.

6 Working quickly, spread the remainder over the top and sides. Sprinkle with icing sugar and decorate with chocolate curls.

CHOCOLATE BRANDY SNAP GATEAU

SERVES 8

225g/8oz plain dark chocolate, chopped
225g/8oz/1 cup unsalted butter, softened
200g/7oz/generous 1 cup dark muscovado sugar
6 eggs, separated
5ml/1 tsp vanilla essence
150g/5oz/1¼ cups ground hazelnuts
60ml/4 tbsp fresh white breadcrumbs
finely grated rind of 1 large orange
1 quantity Chocolate Ganache, for filling and frosting (omit jelly)
icing sugar, for dusting

FOR THE BRANDY SNAPS

50g/2oz/¼ cup unsalted butter
50g/2oz/¼ cup caster sugar
75g/3oz/⅓ cup golden syrup
50g/2oz/½ cup plain flour
5ml/1 tsp brandy

1 Preheat oven to 180°C/350°F/Gas 4. Grease two 20 cm/8 in sandwich cake tins and line the base of each with non-stick baking paper. Melt the chocolate and set aside to cool slightly.

2 Cream the butter with the sugar in a mixing bowl until pale and fluffy. Beat in the egg yolks and vanilla essence. Add the chocolate and mix thoroughly.

3 In a clean, grease-free bowl, whisk the egg whites to soft peaks, then fold them into the chocolate mixture with the ground hazelnuts, breadcrumbs and orange rind.

4 Divide the cake mixture between the prepared tins and smooth the tops. Bake for 25–30 minutes or until well risen and firm. Turn out on to wire racks. Leave the oven on.

5 Make the brandy snaps. Line two baking sheets with non-stick baking paper. Melt the butter, sugar and syrup together.

6 Stir the butter mixture until smooth. Remove from the heat and stir in the flour and brandy.

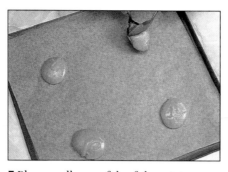

7 Place small spoonfuls of the mixture well apart on the baking sheets and bake for 8–10 minutes, until golden. Cool for a few seconds until firm enough to lift on to a wire rack.

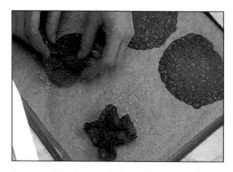

8 Immediately pinch the edges of each brandy snap to create a frilled effect. If the biscuits become too firm, soften them briefly in the oven.

9 Sandwich the cake layers together with half the chocolate ganache, transfer to a plate and spread the remaining ganache on the top. Arrange the brandy snaps over the gâteau and dust with icing sugar.

COOK'S TIP

To save time, you could use ready-made brandy snaps. Simply warm them for a few minutes in the oven until they are pliable enough to shape. Or use as they are, filling them with cream, and arranging them so that they fan out from the centre of the gâteau.

CHOCOLATE COCONUT ROULADE

4 Scrape the mixture into the prepared tin, taking it right into the corners. Smooth the surface with a palette knife, then bake for 20–25 minutes or until well risen and springy to the touch.

5 Turn the cooked roulade out on to the sugar-dusted greaseproof paper and carefully peel off the lining paper. Cover with a damp, clean dish towel and leave to cool completely.

6 Make the filling. Whisk the cream with the whisky in a bowl until the mixture just holds it shape, grate the creamed coconut and stir in with the sugar.

SERVES 8

115g / 4oz / ½ cup caster sugar
5 eggs, separated
50g / 2oz / ½ cup cocoa powder

FOR THE FILLING
300ml / ½ pint / 1¼ cups double cream
45ml / 3 tbsp whisky
or brandy
50g / 2oz piece solid creamed
coconut
30ml / 2 tbsp caster sugar

FOR THE TOPPING
a piece of fresh coconut
dark chocolate for curls

1 Preheat oven to 180°C/350°F/Gas 4. Grease a 33 x 23 cm/13 x 9 in Swiss roll tin. Lay a large sheet of greaseproof paper or non-stick baking paper on the work surface and dust it evenly with 30ml/ 2 tbsp of the caster sugar.

2 Place the egg yolks in a heatproof bowl. Add the remaining caster sugar and whisk with a hand-held electric mixer until the mixture is thick enough to leave a trail. Sift the cocoa over, then fold in carefully and evenly with a metal spoon.

3 Whisk the egg whites in a clean, grease-free bowl until they form soft peaks. Fold about 15ml/1 tbsp of the whites into the chocolate mixture to lighten it, then fold in the rest evenly.

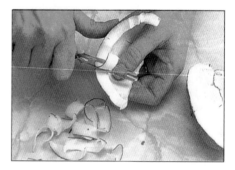

7 Uncover the sponge and spread about three-quarters of the cream mixture to the edges. Roll up carefully from a long side. Transfer to a plate, pipe or spoon the remaining cream mixture on top. Use a vegetable peeler to make coconut and chocolate curls and pile on the cake.

WHITE CHOCOLATE CAPPUCCINO GATEAU

SERVES 8

4 eggs
115g/4oz/½ cup caster sugar
15ml/1 tbsp strong black coffee
2.5ml/½ tsp vanilla essence
115g/4oz/1 cup plain flour
75g/3oz white chocolate, coarsely grated

FOR THE FILLING

120ml/4fl oz/½ cup double cream
15ml/1 tbsp coffee liqueur

FOR THE FROSTING AND TOPPING

15ml/1 tbsp coffee liqueur
1 quantity Chocolate Frosting, using white chocolate and 225g/8oz/2 cups icing sugar

white chocolate curls
cocoa powder or ground cinnamon, for dusting

1 Preheat oven to 180°C/350°F/Gas 4. Grease two 18 cm/7 in round sandwich cake tins and line the base of each with non-stick baking paper.

2 Combine the eggs, caster sugar, coffee and vanilla essence in a large heatproof bowl. Place over a saucepan of hot water and whisk until pale and thick.

3 Sift half the flour over the mixture; fold in gently and evenly. Fold in the remaining flour with the grated white chocolate.

4 Divide the mixture between the prepared tins and smooth level. Bake for 20–25 minutes, until firm and golden brown, then turn out on wire racks and leave to cool completely.

5 Make the filling. Whip the cream with the coffee liqueur in a bowl until it holds its shape. Spread over one of the cakes, then place the second layer on top.

6 Stir the coffee liqueur into the frosting. Spread over the top and sides of the cake, swirling with a palette knife. Top with curls of white chocolate and dust with cocoa or cinnamon. Transfer the cake to a serving plate and set aside until the frosting has set. Serve the gâteau on the day it was made, if possible.

WHITE CHOCOLATE CELEBRATION CAKE

SERVES 40–50

900g / 2lb / 8 cups plain flour
2.5ml / ½ tsp salt
20ml / 4 tsp bicarbonate of soda
450g / 1lb white chocolate, chopped
475ml / 16fl oz / 2 cups whipping cream
450g / 1lb / 2 cups unsalted butter, softened
900g / 2lb / 4 cups caster sugar
12 eggs
20ml / 4 tsp lemon essence
grated rind of 2 lemons
335ml / 11fl oz / 1⅓ cups buttermilk
lemon curd, for filling
chocolate leaves, to decorate

FOR THE LEMON SYRUP
200g / 7oz / scant 1 cup granulated sugar
250ml / 8fl oz / 1 cup water
60ml / 4 tbsp lemon juice

FOR THE BUTTERCREAM
675g / 1½lb white chocolate chopped
1kg / 2¼lb cream cheese, softened
500g / 1¼lb / 2½ cups unsalted butter, at room temperature
60ml / 4 tbsp lemon juice
5ml / 1 tsp lemon essence

1 Divide all the ingredients into two equal batches, so that the quantities are more manageable. Use each batch to make one cake. Preheat oven to 180°C / 350°F / Gas 4. Grease a 30 cm / 12 in round cake tin. Base-line with non-stick baking paper. Sift the flour, salt and bicarbonate of soda into a bowl and set aside. Melt the chocolate and cream in a saucepan over a medium heat, stirring until smooth. Set aside to cool to room temperature.

VARIATION

For a summer celebration, decorate the cake with raspberries and white chocolate petals. To make the petals, you will need about 20 x 7.5 cm / 3 in foil squares. Spread melted white chocolate thinly over each piece of foil, so that it resembles a rose petal. Before the chocolate sets, bend the foil up to emphasize the petal shape. When set, peel away the foil.

2 Beat the butter until creamy, then add the sugar and beat for 2–3 minutes. Beat in the eggs, then slowly beat in the melted chocolate, lemon essence and rind. Gradually add the flour mixture, alternately with the buttermilk, to make a smooth pouring mixture. Pour into the tin and bake for 1 hour or until a skewer inserted in the cake comes out clean.

3 Cool in the tin for 10 minutes, then invert the cake on a wire rack and cool completely. Wrap in clear film until ready to assemble. Using the second batch of ingredients, make another cake in the same way.

4 Make the lemon syrup. In a small saucepan, combine the sugar and water. Over a medium heat, bring to the boil, stirring until the sugar dissolves. Remove from the heat, stir in the lemon juice and cool completely. Store in an airtight container until required.

5 Make the buttercream. Melt the chocolate. Cool slightly. Beat the cream cheese in a bowl until smooth. Gradually beat in the cooled white chocolate, then the butter, lemon juice and essence. Chill.

6 Split each cake in half. Spoon syrup over each layer, let it soak in, then repeat. Spread the bottom half of each cake with lemon curd and replace the tops.

7 Gently beat the buttercream in a bowl until creamy. Spread a quarter over the top of one of the filled cakes. Place the second filled cake on top. Spread a small amount of softened butter over the top and sides of the cake to create a smooth, crumb-free surface. Chill for 15 minutes, so that the buttercream sets a little.

8 Place the cake on a serving plate. Set aside a quarter of the remaining buttercream for piping, then spread the rest evenly over the top and sides of the filled cake.

9 Spoon the reserved buttercream into a large icing bag fitted with a small star tip. Pipe a shell pattern around the rim of the cake. Decorate with chocolate leaves, made with dark or white chocolate (or a mixture) and fresh flowers.

RICH CHOCOLATE LEAF GATEAU

SERVES 8

*75g/3oz plain dark chocolate, broken
into squares
150ml/¼ pint/⅔ cup milk
175g/6oz/¾ cup unsalted butter, softened
250g/9oz/1⅓ cups light muscovado sugar
3 eggs
250g/9oz/2¼ cups plain flour
10ml/2 tsp baking powder
75ml/5 tbsp single cream*

FOR THE FILLING AND TOPPING

*60ml/4 tbsp raspberry conserve
1 quantity Chocolate Ganache
dark and white chocolate leaves*

1 Preheat oven to 190°C/375°F/Gas 5.
Grease and base-line two 22 cm/8½ in
sandwich cake tins. Melt the chocolate
with the milk over a low heat and allow
to cool slightly.

2 Cream the butter with the light
muscovado sugar in a mixing bowl until
light and fluffy. Add the eggs, one at a
time, beating well after each addition.
3 Sift the flour and baking powder over
the mixture and fold in gently but
thoroughly. Stir in the chocolate mixture
and the cream, mixing until smooth.
Divide between the prepared tins and
level the tops.

4 Bake the cakes for 30–35 minutes or
until they are well risen and firm to the
touch. Cool in the tins for a few minutes,
then turn out on to wire racks.

5 Sandwich the cake layers together with
the raspberry conserve. Spread the
chocolate ganache over the cake and
swirl with a knife. Place the cake on a
serving plate, then decorate with the
chocolate leaves.

CARIBBEAN CHOCOLATE RING WITH RUM SYRUP

SERVES 8–10

115g/4oz/½ cup unsalted butter
115g/4oz/¾ cup light muscovado sugar
2 eggs, beaten
2 ripe bananas, mashed
30ml/2 tbsp desiccated coconut
30ml/2 tbsp soured cream
115g/4oz/1 cup self-raising flour
45ml/3 tbsp cocoa powder
2.5ml/½ tsp bicarbonate of soda

FOR THE SYRUP

115g/4oz/½ cup caster sugar
30ml/2 tbsp dark rum
50g/2oz plain dark chocolate, chopped

TO DECORATE

mixture of tropical fruits, such as mango,
pawpaw, starfruit and cape gooseberries
chocolate shapes or curls

1 Preheat oven to 180°C/350°F/Gas 4. Grease a 1.5 litre/2½ pint/6¼ cup ring tin with butter.

2 Cream the butter and sugar in a bowl until light and fluffy. Add the eggs gradually, beating well, then mix in the bananas, coconut and soured cream.

3 Sift the flour, cocoa and bicarbonate of soda over the mixture and fold in thoroughly and evenly.

4 Tip into the prepared tin and spread evenly. Bake for 45–50 minutes, until firm to the touch. Cool for 10 minutes in the tin, then turn out to finish cooling on a wire rack.

5 For the syrup, place the sugar in a small pan. Add 60ml/4 tbsp water and heat gently, stirring occasionally until dissolved. Bring to the boil and boil rapidly, without stirring, for 2 minutes. Remove from the heat.

6 Add the rum and chocolate to the syrup and stir until the mixture is melted and smooth, then spoon evenly over the top and sides of the cake.

7 Decorate the ring with tropical fruits and chocolate shapes or curls.

WHITE CHOCOLATE MOUSSE AND STRAWBERRY LAYER CAKE

4 Make the mousse filling. In a medium saucepan over a low heat, melt the chocolate and cream until smooth, stirring frequently. Stir in the rum or strawberry-flavoured liqueur and pour into a bowl. Chill until just set. With a wire whisk, whip lightly.

5 Assemble the cake. With a serrated knife, slice both cake layers in half, making four layers. Place one layer on the plate and spread one third of the mousse on top. Arrange one third of the sliced strawberries over the mousse. Place the second layer on top and spread with another third of the mousse. Arrange another third of the sliced strawberries over the mousse. Place the third layer on top and spread with the remaining mousse. Cover with the remaining sliced strawberries. Top with the last cake layer.

6 Whip the cream with the rum or liqueur until firm peaks form. Spread about half the whipped cream over the top and the sides of the cake. Spoon the remaining cream into a decorating bag fitted with a medium star tip and pipe scrolls on top of the cake. Decorate with the remaining sliced strawberries, pressing half of them into the cream on the side of the cake and arranging the rest on top.

SERVES 10

*115g/4oz fine white chocolate, chopped into
small pieces*
120ml/4fl oz/½ cup double cream
120ml/4fl oz/½ cup milk
15ml/1 tbsp rum or vanilla essence
115g/4oz/½ cup unsalted butter, softened
175g/6oz/¾ cup granulated sugar
3 eggs
225g/8oz/2 cups plain flour
10ml/2 tsp baking powder
pinch of salt
*675g/1½lb fresh strawberries, sliced, plus
extra for decoration*
*750ml/1¼ pints/3 cups whipping
cream*
*30ml/2 tbsp rum or strawberry-flavoured
liqueur*

WHITE CHOCOLATE MOUSSE FILLING

*250g/9oz white chocolate, chopped into
small pieces*
350ml/12fl oz/1½ cups double cream
*30ml/2 tbsp rum or strawberry-flavoured
liqueur*

1 Preheat oven to 180°C/350°F/Gas 4. Grease and flour two 23 x 5 cm/9 x 2 in cake tins. Line the base of the tins with non-stick baking paper. Melt the chocolate and cream in a double boiler over a low heat, stirring until smooth. Stir in the milk and rum or vanilla essence, and set aside to cool.

2 In a large mixing bowl, beat the butter and sugar with a hand-held electric mixer for 3–5 minutes, until light and creamy, scraping the sides of the bowl occasionally. Add the eggs one at a time, beating well after each addition. In a small bowl, stir together the flour, baking powder and salt. Alternately add flour and melted chocolate to the egg mixture in batches, until just blended. Pour the mixture into the tins and spread evenly.

3 Bake for 20–25 minutes, until a skewer inserted in the cake comes out clean. Cool in the tin for 10 minutes, then turn cakes out on to a wire rack, peel off the paper and cool completely.

CHOCOLATE CHESTNUT ROULADE

SERVES 10–12

*175g/6oz bittersweet chocolate, chopped into
small pieces
30ml/2 tbsp cocoa powder, sifted
60ml/4 tbsp hot strong coffee or espresso
6 eggs, separated
75g/3oz/6 tbsp caster sugar
pinch of cream of tartar
5ml/1 tsp pure vanilla essence
cocoa powder, for dusting
glacé chestnuts, to decorate*

CHESTNUT CREAM FILLING

*475ml/16fl oz/2 cups double cream
30ml/2 tbsp rum or coffee-flavoured liqueur
350g/12oz/1½ cups canned sweetened
chestnut purée
115g/4oz bittersweet chocolate, grated*

4 Dust a dish towel with cocoa. Turn the cake out on to the towel immediately and remove the paper. Trim off any crisp edges. Starting at a narrow end, roll the cake and towel together Swiss roll fashion. Cool completely.

5 Make the filling. Whip the cream and rum or liqueur until soft peaks form. Beat a spoonful of cream into the chestnut purée to lighten it, then fold in the remaining cream and grated chocolate. Set aside a quarter of this mixture for the decoration. Unroll the cake and spread chestnut cream to within 2.5 cm/1 in of the edge.

6 Using a dish towel to lift the cake, carefully roll it up again. Place seam-side down on a serving plate. Spread some of the reserved chestnut cream over the top and use the rest for piped rosettes. Decorate with the glacé chestnuts.

1 Preheat oven to 180°C/350°F/Gas 4. Lightly grease the base and sides of a 39 x 27 x 2.5 cm/15½ x 10½ x 1 in Swiss roll tin. Line with non-stick baking paper, allowing a 2.5 cm/1 in overhang. Melt the chocolate. Dissolve the cocoa in the hot coffee to make a paste. Set aside.

2 Using a hand-held mixer, beat the egg yolks with half the sugar in a mixing bowl until pale and thick. Slowly beat in the melted chocolate and cocoa-coffee paste until just blended. In a separate bowl, beat the egg whites and cream of tartar until stiff peaks form. Sprinkle the remaining sugar over the whites in two batches and beat until the whites are stiff and glossy, then beat in the vanilla essence.

3 Stir a spoonful of the whites into the chocolate mixture to lighten it, then fold in the rest. Spoon into the tin. Bake for 20–25 minutes or until the cake springs back when touched with a fingertip.

CHOCOLATE REDCURRANT TORTE

SERVES 8–10

115g/4oz/½ cup unsalted butter, softened
115g/4oz/⅔ cup dark muscovado sugar
2 eggs
150ml/¼ pint/⅔ cup soured cream
150g/5oz/1¼ cups self-raising flour
5ml/1 tsp baking powder
50g/2oz/½ cup cocoa powder
75g/3oz/¾ cup stemmed redcurrants, plus
115g/4oz/1 cup redcurrant sprigs, to decorate

FOR THE ICING

150g/5oz plain chocolate, chopped into small pieces
45ml/3 tbsp redcurrant jelly
30ml/2 tbsp dark rum
120ml/4fl oz/½ cup double cream

1 Preheat oven to 180°C/350°F/Gas 4. Grease a 1.2 litre/2 pint/5 cup ring tin and dust lightly with flour. Cream the butter with the sugar in a mixing bowl until pale and fluffy. Beat in the eggs and soured cream until thoroughly mixed.

2 Sift the flour, baking powder and cocoa over the mixture, then fold in lightly and evenly. Fold in the stemmed redcurrants. Spoon the mixture into the prepared tin and smooth the surface level. Bake for 40–50 minutes or until well risen and firm. Turn out on to a wire rack and leave to cool completely.

3 Make the icing. Mix the chocolate, redcurrant jelly and rum in a heatproof bowl. Set the bowl over simmering water and heat gently, stirring occasionally, until melted. Remove from the heat and cool to room temperature, then add the double cream, a little at a time. Mix well.

4 Transfer the cooked cake to a serving plate. Spoon the icing evenly over the cake, allowing it to drizzle down the sides. Decorate with redcurrant sprigs just before serving.

COOK'S TIP

Use a decorative gugelhupf tin or mould, if you have one. When preparing it, add a little cocoa powder to the flour used for dusting the greased tin, as this will prevent the cooked chocolate cake from being streaked with white.

CHOCOLATE BOX WITH CARAMEL MOUSSE AND BERRIES

SERVES 8–10

*275g / 10oz plain chocolate, chopped into
small pieces*

FOR THE CARAMEL MOUSSE

*4 x 50g / 2oz chocolate-coated caramel bars,
coarsely chopped*

25ml / 1½ tbsp milk or water

350ml / 12fl oz / 1½ cups double cream

1 egg white

FOR THE CARAMEL SHARDS

115g / 4oz / ½ cup granulated sugar

60ml / 4 tbsp water

FOR THE TOPPING

*115g / 4oz fine quality white chocolate,
chopped into small pieces*

350ml / 12fl oz / 1½ cups double cream

*450g / 1lb mixed berries or cut up fruits such
as raspberries, strawberries, blackberries or
sliced nectarine and orange segments*

<u>1</u> Prepare the chocolate box. Turn a
23 cm / 9 in square baking tin bottom-
side up. Mould a piece of foil around the
tin, then turn it right side up and line it
with the foil, pressing against the edges to
make the foil as smooth as possible.

<u>2</u> Place the plain chocolate in a heatproof
bowl over a saucepan of simmering water
Stir until the chocolate has melted and is
smooth. Immediately pour the melted
chocolate into the lined tin. Tilt to coat
the bottom and sides evenly, keeping the
top edges of the sides as straight as
possible. As the chocolate coats the sides,
tilt the pan again to coat the corners and
sides once more. Chill until firm.

<u>3</u> Place the caramel bars and milk or
water in a heatproof bowl. Place over a
pan of simmering water and stir until
melted. Remove the bowl from the heat
and cool for 10 minutes, stirring
occasionally.

<u>4</u> Using a hand-held electric mixer, whip
the cream in a bowl until soft peaks form.
Stir a spoonful of the whipped cream into
the caramel mixture to lighten it, then
fold in the remaining cream. In another
bowl beat the egg white until just stiff.
Fold the egg white into the mousse
mixture. Pour into the box. Chill for
several hours or overnight, until set.

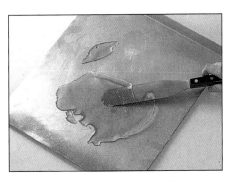

<u>5</u> Meanwhile, make the caramel shards.
Lightly oil a baking sheet. In a small pan
over a low heat, dissolve the sugar in the
water, swirling the pan gently. Increase
the heat and boil the mixture for 4–5
minutes, until the sugar begins to turn a
pale golden colour. Protecting your hand
with an oven glove, immediately pour the
mixture on to the oiled sheet. Tilt the
sheet to distribute the caramel in an even
layer. (*Do not touch – caramel is dangerously
hot.*) Cool completely, then using a metal
palette knife, lift the caramel off the
baking sheet and break into pieces.

<u>6</u> Make the topping. Combine the white
chocolate and 120ml / 4fl oz / ½ cup of the
cream in a small pan and melt over a low
heat until smooth, stirring frequently.
Strain into a medium bowl and cool to
room temperature, stirring occasionally.
In another bowl, beat the remaining
cream with a hand-held electric mixer,
until firm peaks form. Stir a spoonful of
cream into the white chocolate mixture,
then gently fold in the remaining
whipped cream.

<u>7</u> Using the foil as a guide, remove the
mousse-filled box from the tin and peel
the foil carefully from the sides, then the
bottom. Slide the box gently on to a
serving plate.

<u>8</u> Spoon the chocolate-cream mixture
into a piping bag fitted with a medium
star tip. Pipe a decorative design of
rosettes or shells over the surface of the
set mousse. Decorate the cream-topped
box with the mixed berries or cut up
fruits and the caramel shards.

Dark Chocolate Ravioli with White Chocolate and Cream Cheese Filling

Serves 4

175g/6oz/1½ cups plain flour
25g/1oz/¼ cup cocoa powder
salt
30ml/2 tbsp icing sugar
2 large eggs, beaten
15ml/1 tbsp olive oil
single cream and grated chocolate, to serve

For the Filling

175g/6oz white chocolate, chopped
350g/12oz/3 cups cream cheese
1 egg, plus 1 beaten egg to seal

1 Make the pasta. Sift the flour with the cocoa, salt and icing sugar on to a work surface. Make a well in the centre and pour the eggs and oil in. Mix together with your fingers. Knead until smooth. Alternatively, make the dough in a food processor, then knead by hand. Cover and rest for at least 30 minutes.

2 To make the filling, melt the white chocolate in a heatproof bowl placed over a pan of simmering water. Cool slightly. Beat the cream cheese in a bowl, then beat in the chocolate and eggs. Spoon into a piping bag fitted with a plain nozzle.

3 Cut the dough in half and wrap one portion in clear film. Roll the pasta out thinly to a rectangle on a lightly floured surface, or use a pasta machine. Cover with a clean damp dish towel and repeat with the remaining pasta.

4 Pipe small mounds (about 5ml/1 tsp) of filling in even rows, spacing them at 4 cm/1½ in intervals across one piece of the dough. Using a pastry brush, brush the spaces of dough between the mounds with beaten egg.

5 Using a rolling pin, lift the remaining sheet of pasta over the dough with the filling. Press down firmly between the pockets of filling, pushing out any trapped air. Cut the filled chocolate pasta into rounds with a serrated ravioli cutter or sharp knife. Transfer to a floured dish towel. Leave for 1 hour to dry out, ready for cooking.

6 Bring a frying pan of water to the boil and add the ravioli a few at a time, stirring to prevent them sticking together. (Adding a few drops of a bland oil to the water will help, too.) Simmer gently for 3–5 minutes, remove with a perforated spoon and serve with a generous splash of single cream and grated chocolate.

CHOCOLATE ALMOND MERINGUE PIE

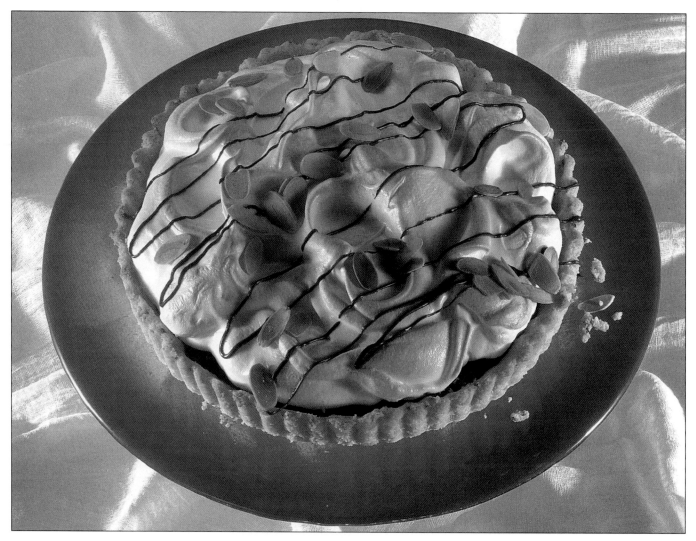

SERVES 6

175g/6oz/1½ cups plain flour
50g/2oz/½ cup ground rice
150g/5oz/⅔ cup unsalted butter
finely grated rind of 1 orange
1 egg yolk
*flaked almonds and melted plain dark
chocolate, to decorate*

FOR THE FILLING

*150g/5oz plain dark chocolate, chopped into
small pieces*
50g/2oz/4 tbsp unsalted butter, softened
75g/3oz/6 tbsp caster sugar
10ml/2 tsp cornflour
4 egg yolks
75g/3oz/¾ cup ground almonds

FOR THE MERINGUE

3 egg whites
150g/5oz/⅔ cup caster sugar

1 Sift the flour and ground rice into a bowl. Rub in the butter until the mixture resembles breadcrumbs. Stir in the orange rind. Add the egg yolks; bring the dough together. Roll out and use to line a 23 cm/9 in round flan tin. Chill.

2 Preheat oven to 190°C/375°F/Gas 5. Prick the pastry base, cover with grease-proof paper weighed down with baking beans and bake blind for 10 minutes.

3 Make the filling. Melt the chocolate, then cream the butter with the sugar in a bowl, and beat in the cornflour and egg yolks. Fold in the almonds, then the melted chocolate. Remove the paper and beans from the pastry case and add the filling. Bake for a further 10 minutes.

4 Make the meringue. Whisk the egg whites in a clean, grease-free bowl until stiff, then gradually whisk in about half the caster sugar. Fold in the remaining sugar with a metal spoon.

5 Spoon the meringue over the chocolate filling, lifting it up with the back of the spoon to form peaks. Reduce the oven temperature to 180°C/350°F/Gas 4 and bake the pie for 15–20 minutes or until the topping is pale gold. Serve warm, scattered with the almonds and drizzled with the melted chocolate.

MAGIC CHOCOLATE MUD PUDDING

SERVES 4

50g/2oz/4 tbsp butter, plus extra for greasing
90g/3½oz/scant 1 cup self-raising flour
5ml/1 tsp ground cinnamon
75ml/5 tbsp cocoa powder
200g/7oz/generous 1 cup light muscovado or demerara sugar
475ml/16fl oz/2 cups milk
crème fraîche, Greek-style yogurt or vanilla ice cream, to serve

1 Preheat oven to 180°C/350°F/Gas 4. Prepare the dish: use the extra butter to grease a 1.5 litre/2½ pint/6¼ cup ovenproof dish. Place the dish on a baking sheet and set aside.

2 Sift the flour and ground cinnamon into a bowl. Sift in 15ml/1 tbsp of the cocoa and mix well.

3 Place the butter in a saucepan. Add 115g/4oz/½ cup of the sugar and 150ml/¼ pint/⅔ cup of the milk. Heat gently without boiling, stirring from time to time, until the butter has melted and all the sugar has dissolved. Remove the pan from the heat.

4 Stir in the flour mixture, mixing evenly. Pour the mixture into the prepared dish and level the surface.

5 Mix the remaining sugar and cocoa in a bowl, then sprinkle over the pudding mixture.

6 Pour the remaining milk evenly over the pudding.

7 Bake for 45–50 minutes or until the sponge has risen to the top and is firm to the touch. Serve hot, with the crème fraîche, yogurt or ice cream.

CHOCOLATE CREPES WITH PLUMS AND PORT

2 Meanwhile, make the filling. Halve and stone the plums. Place them in a saucepan and add the sugar and water. Bring to the boil, then lower the heat, cover, and simmer for about 10 minutes or until the plums are tender. Stir in the port, taking care not to break up the plums, then simmer for a further 30 seconds. Remove from the heat and keep warm.

3 Have ready a sheet of non-stick baking paper. Heat a crêpe pan, grease it lightly with a little oil, then pour in just enough batter to cover the base of the pan, swirling to coat evenly. Cook until the crêpe has set, then flip it over to cook the other side. Slide the crêpe out on to the sheet of paper, then cook 9–11 more crêpes in the same way. It should not be necessary to add more oil to the pan, but if the crêpes start to stick, add a very light coating.

4 Make the sauce. Combine the chocolate and cream in a saucepan. Heat gently, stirring until smooth. Add the port and heat gently, stirring, for 1 minute.

5 Divide the plum filling among the crêpes, add a dollop of crème fraîche or Greek-style yogurt to each and roll them up carefully. Serve in individual bowls, with the chocolate sauce spooned over the top of each portion.

SERVES 6

50g / 2oz plain chocolate, chopped into
small pieces
200ml / 7fl oz / scant 1 cup milk
120ml / 4fl oz / ½ cup single cream
30ml / 2 tbsp cocoa powder
115g / 4oz / 1 cup plain flour
2 eggs
oil, for frying

FOR THE FILLING

500g / 1¼lb red or golden plums
50g / 2oz / ¼ cup caster sugar
30ml / 2 tbsp water
30ml / 2 tbsp port
150g / 5oz / ¾ cup crème fraîche or
Greek-style yogurt

FOR THE SAUCE

150g / 5oz plain chocolate, chopped into
small pieces
175ml / 6fl oz / ¾ cup double cream
15ml / 1 tbsp port

1 Make the crêpe batter. Place the chocolate in a saucepan with the milk. Heat gently, stirring occasionally, until the chocolate has dissolved. Pour the chocolate and milk mixture into a blender or food processor and add the cream, cocoa, flour and eggs. (If the blender or food processor is a small one, it may be necessary to do this in batches.) Process until smooth, then tip into a jug and chill for 30 minutes.

STEAMED CHOCOLATE AND FRUIT PUDDINGS WITH CHOCOLATE SYRUP

SERVES 4

115g / 4oz / ⅔ cup dark muscovado sugar
1 eating apple
75g / 3oz / ¾ cup cranberries, thawed if frozen
115g / 4oz / ½ cup soft margarine
2 eggs
115g / 4oz / ½ cup self-raising flour
45ml / 3 tbsp cocoa powder

FOR THE CHOCOLATE SYRUP

115g / 4oz plain chocolate, chopped
30ml / 2 tbsp clear honey
15ml / ½oz / 1 tbsp unsalted butter
2.5ml / ½ tsp vanilla essence

1 Prepare a steamer or half fill a saucepan with water and bring it to the boil. Grease four individual pudding basins and sprinkle each one with a little of the muscovado sugar to coat well all over.

2 Peel and core the apple. Dice it into a bowl, add the cranberries and mix well. Divide the fruit among the prepared pudding basins.

3 Place the remaining muscovado sugar in a mixing bowl. Add the margarine, eggs, flour and cocoa. Beat until combined and smooth.

4 Spoon the mixture into the basins and cover each with a double thickness of foil. Steam for about 45 minutes, topping up the boiling water as required, until the puddings are well risen and firm.

5 Make the syrup. Mix the chocolate, honey, butter and vanilla essence in a small saucepan. Heat gently, stirring until melted and smooth.

6 Run a knife around the edge of each pudding to loosen it, then turn out on to individual plates. Serve at once, with the chocolate syrup.

CHOCOLATE SOUFFLE CREPES

MAKES 12 CREPES

75g / 3oz / ¾ cup plain flour
15ml / 1 tbsp cocoa powder
5ml / 1 tsp caster sugar
pinch of salt
5ml / 1 tsp ground cinnamon
2 eggs
175ml / 6fl oz / ¾ cup milk
5ml / 1 tsp vanilla essence
50g / 2oz / 4 tbsp unsalted butter,
melted
raspberries, pineapple and mint sprigs,
to decorate

FOR THE PINEAPPLE SYRUP

½ medium pineapple, peeled, cored and
finely chopped
120ml / 4fl oz / ½ cup water
30ml / 2 tbsp natural maple syrup
5ml / 1 tsp cornflour
½ cinnamon stick
30ml / 2 tbsp rum

FOR THE SOUFFLE FILLING

250g / 9oz bittersweet chocolate, chopped into
small pieces
75ml / 3fl oz / ⅓ cup double cream
3 eggs, separated
25g / 1oz / 2 tbsp caster sugar

<u>1</u> Prepare the syrup. In a saucepan over a medium heat, bring the pineapple, water, maple syrup, cornflour and cinnamon stick to the boil. Simmer for 2–3 minutes, until the sauce thickens, whisking frequently. Remove from the heat and discard the cinnamon. Pour into a bowl, and stir in the rum. Cool, then chill.

COOK'S TIP
You might be able to find ready-made crepes in the shops, which will save time.

<u>2</u> Prepare the crêpes. Sift the flour, cocoa, sugar, salt and cinnamon into a bowl. Stir, then make a well in the centre. In a bowl, beat the eggs, milk and vanilla. Gradually add to the well in the flour mixture, whisking in flour from the side of the bowl to form a smooth batter. Stir in half the melted butter and pour into a jug. Allow to stand for 1 hour.

<u>3</u> Heat an 18–20 cm / 7–8 in crêpe pan. Brush with butter. Stir the batter. Pour 45ml / 3 tbsp batter into the pan; swirl the pan to cover the bottom. Cook over a medium-high heat for 1–2 minutes until the bottom is golden. Turn over and cook for 30–45 seconds, then turn on to a plate. Stack between sheets of non-stick baking paper and set aside.

<u>4</u> Prepare the filling. In a saucepan over a medium heat, melt the chocolate and cream until smooth, stirring frequently.

<u>5</u> In a bowl, with a hand-held electric mixer, beat the yolks with half the sugar for 3–5 minutes, until light and creamy. Gradually beat in the chocolate mixture. Allow to cool. In a separate bowl with cleaned beaters, beat the egg whites until soft peaks form. Gradually beat in the remaining sugar until stiff peaks form. Beat a large spoonful of whites in to the chocolate mixture to lighten it, then fold in the remaining whites.

<u>6</u> Preheat oven to 200°C / 400°F / Gas 6. Lay a crêpe on a plate, bottom side up. Spoon a little soufflé mixture on to the crêpe, spreading it to the edge. Fold the bottom half over the soufflé mixture, then fold in half again to form a filled triangle. Place on a buttered baking sheet. Repeat with the remaining crêpes. Brush the tops with melted butter and bake for 15–20 minutes, until the filling has souffléd. Decorate with raspberries, pineapple pieces and mint and serve with the syrup.

VARIATION
For a simpler version of the crêpes, just serve with a spoonful of maple syrup rather than making the pineapple syrup.

Chocolate and Orange Scotch Pancakes

Serves 4

115g / 4oz / 1 cup self-raising flour
30ml / 2 tbsp cocoa powder
2 eggs
50g / 2oz plain chocolate, chopped into
small pieces
200ml / 7fl oz / scant 1 cup milk
finely grated rind of 1 orange
30ml / 2 tbsp orange juice
butter or oil, for frying
chocolate curls, to decorate

For the Sauce

2 large oranges
25g / 1oz / 2 tbsp unsalted butter
45ml / 3 tbsp light muscovado sugar
250ml / 8fl oz / 1 cup crème fraîche
30ml / 2 tbsp Grand Marnier or
Cointreau

1 Sift the flour and cocoa into a bowl and make a well in the centre. Add the eggs and beat well, gradually incorporating the surrounding dry ingredients to make a smooth mixture.

2 Mix the chocolate and milk in a saucepan. Heat gently until the chocolate has melted, then beat into the mixture until smooth and bubbly. Stir in the orange rind and juice to make a batter.

3 Heat a large heavy-based frying pan or griddle. Grease with a little butter or oil. Drop large spoonfuls of batter on to the hot surface, leaving room for spreading. Cook over a moderate heat. When the pancakes are lightly browned underneath and bubbly on top, flip over to cook the other side. Slide on to a plate and keep hot, then make more in the same way.

4 Make the sauce. Grate the rind of 1 orange into a bowl and set aside. Peel both oranges, taking care to remove all the pith, then slice the flesh fairly thinly.

5 Heat the butter and sugar in a wide, shallow pan over a low heat, stirring until the sugar dissolves. Stir in the crème fraîche and heat gently.

6 Add the pancakes and orange slices to the sauce, heat gently for 1–2 minutes, then spoon over the liqueur. Sprinkle with the reserved orange rind. Scatter over the chocolate curls and serve the pancakes at once.

PUFFY PEARS

SERVES 4

225g/8oz puff pastry, thawed if frozen
2 pears, peeled
2 squares plain chocolate, roughly chopped
15ml/1 tbsp lemon juice
1 egg, beaten
15ml/1 tbsp caster sugar

1 Roll the pastry into a 25 cm/10 in square on a lightly floured surface. Trim the edges, then cut it into four equal smaller squares. Cover with clear film and set aside.
2 Remove the core from each pear half and pack the gap with the chopped chocolate. Place a pear half, cut-side down, on each piece of pastry and brush them with the lemon juice, to prevent them from going brown.
3 Preheat oven to 190°C/375°F/Gas 5. Cut the pastry into a pear shape, by following the lines of the fruit, leaving a 2.5 cm/1 in border. Use the trimmings to make leaves and brush the pastry border with the beaten egg.
4 Arrange the pastry and pears on a baking sheet. Make deep cuts in the pears, taking care not to cut right through the fruit, and sprinkle them with the sugar. Cook for 20–25 minutes, until lightly browned. Serve hot or cold.

VARIATION

Use apples instead of pears, if preferred. Cut the pastry into 10 cm/4 in rounds. Slice 2 peeled and cored eating apples. Toss with a little lemon juice, drain and arrange on the pastry. Dot with 25g/1oz/2 tbsp butter and chopped milk chocolate. Bake as for Puffy Pears. While still hot, brush the apple slices with warmed redcurrant jelly.

PEARS IN CHOCOLATE FUDGE BLANKETS

SERVES 6

6 ripe eating pears
30ml/2 tbsp lemon juice
75g/3oz/6 tbsp caster sugar
300ml/½ pint/1¼ cups water
1 cinnamon stick
FOR THE SAUCE
200ml/7fl oz/scant 1 cup double cream
150g/5oz/scant 1 cup light muscovado sugar
25g/1oz/2tbsp unsalted butter
25g/1oz/2 tbsp golden syrup
120ml/4fl oz/½ cup milk
200g/7oz plain dark chocolate, broken into squares

1 Peel the pears thinly, leaving the stalks on. Scoop out the cores from the base. Brush the cut surfaces with lemon juice to prevent them from browning.
2 Place the sugar and water in a large saucepan. Heat gently until the sugar dissolves. Add the pears and cinnamon stick with any remaining lemon juice, and, if necessary, a little more water, so that the pears are almost covered.
3 Bring to the boil, then lower the heat, cover the pan and simmer the pears gently for 15–20 minutes or until they are just tender when pierced with a slim skewer.
4 Meanwhile, make the sauce. Place the cream, sugar, butter, golden syrup and milk in a heavy-based saucepan. Heat gently until the sugar has dissolved and the butter and syrup have melted, then bring to the boil. Boil, stirring constantly, for about 5 minutes or until the sauce is thick. Remove from the heat and stir in the chocolate, a few squares at a time, until melted.
5 Using a slotted spoon, transfer the poached pears to a dish. Keep hot. Boil the syrup rapidly to reduce to about 45–60ml/3–4 tbsp. Remove the cinnamon stick and stir the syrup into the chocolate sauce. Serve poured over the pears in individual bowls.

RICH CHOCOLATE BERRY TART WITH BLACKBERRY SAUCE

SERVES 10

115g/4oz/½ cup unsalted butter, softened

115g/4oz/½ cup caster sugar

2.5ml/½ tsp salt

15ml/1 tbsp vanilla essence

50g/2oz/½ cup cocoa powder

175g/6oz/1½ cups plain flour

450g/1 lb fresh berries, for topping

FOR THE CHOCOLATE GANACHE FILLING

475ml/16fl oz/2 cups double cream

150g/5oz/½ cup blackberry or raspberry jelly

225g/8oz bittersweet chocolate, chopped into small pieces

25g/1oz/2 tbsp unsalted butter, cut into small pieces

FOR THE BLACKBERRY SAUCE

225g/8oz fresh or frozen blackberries or raspberries

15ml/1 tbsp lemon juice

30ml/2 tbsp caster sugar

30ml/2 tbsp blackberry- or raspberry-flavoured liqueur

1 In a food processor fitted with a metal blade, process the butter, sugar, salt and vanilla essence until creamy. Add the cocoa and process for 1 minute. Add the flour all at once, then pulse for 10–15 seconds. Place a piece of clear film on the work surface. Turn the dough out on to this, shape into a flat disc and wrap tightly. Chill for 1 hour.

2 Lightly grease a 23 cm/9 in flan tin with a removable base. Let the dough soften for 5–10 minutes, then roll out between two sheets of clear film to a 28 cm/11 in round, about 5 mm/¼ in thick. Peel off the top sheet of clear film and invert the dough into the prepared tin. Ease the dough into the tin, and when in position lift off the clear film.

3 With floured fingers, press the dough on to the base and sides of the tin, then roll the rolling pin over the edge to cut off any excess dough. Prick the base of the dough with a fork. Chill for 1 hour. Preheat oven to 180°C/350°F/Gas 4. Line the pastry case with non-stick baking paper; fill with baking beans and bake blind for 10 minutes. Remove the paper and beans and bake for 5 minutes more, until the pastry is just set. Cool in the tin on a wire rack.

4 Prepare the ganache filling. In a medium saucepan over a medium heat, bring the cream and berry jelly to the boil. Remove from the heat and add the chocolate all at once, stirring until melted and smooth. Stir in the butter until melted, then strain into the cooled tart shell, smoothing the top. Cool the tart completely.

5 Prepare the sauce. Process the berries, lemon juice and sugar in a food processor until smooth. Strain into a small bowl and add the liqueur.

6 To serve, remove the tart from the tin. Place on a serving plate and arrange the berries on top of the tart. With a pastry brush, brush the berries with a little of the blackberry sauce to glaze lightly. Serve the remaining sauce separately.

Chocolate Truffle Tart

Serves 12

115g/4oz/1 cup plain flour
30g/1¼oz/⅓ cup cocoa powder
50g/2oz/¼ cup caster sugar
2.5ml/½ tsp salt
115g/4oz/½ cup unsalted butter, cut into pieces
1 egg yolk
15–30ml/1–2 tbsp iced water
25g/1oz fine quality white or milk chocolate, melted
whipped cream for serving (optional)

For the Truffle Filling
350ml/12fl oz/1½ cups double cream
350g/12oz couverture or fine quality bittersweet chocolate, chopped
50g/2oz/4 tbsp unsalted butter, cut into small pieces
30ml/2 tbsp brandy or liqueur

1 Prepare the pastry. Sift the flour and cocoa into a bowl. In a food processor fitted with a metal blade, process the flour mixture with the sugar and salt. Add the butter and process for 15–20 seconds, until the mixture resembles coarse breadcrumbs.

2 In a bowl, lightly beat the yolk with the iced water. Add to the flour mixture and pulse until the dough begins to stick together. Turn out the dough on to a sheet of clear film. Use the film to help shape the dough into a flat disc. Wrap tightly. Chill for 1–2 hours, until firm.

3 Lightly grease a 23 cm/9 in tart tin with a removable base. Let the dough soften briefly, then roll it out between sheets of waxed paper or clear film to a 28 cm/11 in round, about 5 mm/¼ in thick. Peel off the top sheet and invert the dough into a tart tin. Remove the bottom sheet. Ease the dough into the tin. Prick with a fork. Chill for 1 hour.

4 Preheat oven to 180°C/350°F/Gas 4. Line the tart with foil or non-stick baking paper; fill with baking beans. Bake blind for 5–7 minutes. Lift out the foil with the beans, return the pastry case to the oven and bake for a further 5–7 minutes, until the pastry is just set. Cool completely in the tin on a rack.

5 Prepare the filling. In a medium pan over a medium heat, bring the cream to the boil. Remove the pan from the heat and stir in the chocolate until melted and smooth. Stir in the butter and brandy or liqueur. Strain into the prepared tart shell, tilting the tin slightly to level the surface. Do not touch the surface of the filling or it will spoil the glossy finish.

6 Spoon the melted chocolate into a paper piping bag and cut off the tip. Drop rounds of chocolate over the surface of the tart and use a skewer or toothpick to draw a point gently through the chocolate to produce a marbled effect. Chill for 2–3 hours, until set. To serve, allow the tart to soften slightly at room temperature.

MARBLED CHOCOLATE CHEESECAKE

SERVES 6

50g / 2oz / ½ cup cocoa powder
75ml / 5 tbsp hot water
900g / 2lb cream cheese, at room temperature
200g / 7oz / scant 1 cup caster sugar
4 eggs
5ml / 1 tsp vanilla essence
75g / 3oz digestive biscuits, crushed

<u>1</u> Preheat oven to 180°C/350°F/Gas 4. Line a 20 x 8 cm/8 x 3 in cake tin with greaseproof paper. Grease the paper.
<u>2</u> Sift the cocoa powder into a bowl. Pour over the hot water and stir to dissolve.
<u>3</u> Beat the cheese until smooth, then beat in the sugar, followed by the eggs, one at a time. Do not overmix.
<u>4</u> Divide the mixture evenly between two bowls. Stir the chocolate mixture into one bowl, then add the vanilla essence to the remaining mixture.

<u>5</u> Pour a cup or ladleful of the plain mixture into the centre of the tin; it will spread out into an even layer. Slowly pour over a cupful of chocolate mixture in the centre. Continue to alternate the cake mixtures in this way until both are used up. Draw a thin metal skewer through the cake mixture for a marbled effect.
<u>6</u> Set the tin in a roasting pan and pour in hot water to come 4 cm/1½ in up the sides of the cake tin.

<u>7</u> Bake the cheesecake for about 1½ hours, until the top is golden. (The cake will rise during baking but will sink later.) Cool in the tin on a wire rack.
<u>8</u> Run a knife around the inside edge of the cake. Invert a flat plate over the tin and turn out the cake.

<u>9</u> Sprinkle the crushed biscuits evenly over the cake, gently invert another plate on top, and turn over again. Cover and chill for 3 hours, preferably overnight.

BLACK BOTTOM PIE

SERVES 6–8

250g/9oz/2¼ cups plain flour
150g/5oz/⅔ cup unsalted butter
2 egg yolks
15–30ml/1–2 tbsp iced water

FOR THE FILLING

3 eggs, separated
20ml/4 tsp cornflour
75g/3oz/6 tbsp golden caster sugar
400ml/14fl oz/1⅔ cups milk
150g/5oz plain chocolate, chopped into
small pieces
5ml/1 tsp vanilla essence
1 sachet powdered gelatine
45ml/3 tbsp water
30ml/2 tbsp dark rum

FOR THE TOPPING

175ml/6 fl oz/¾ cup double cream or
whipping cream
chocolate curls

1 Sift the flour into a bowl and rub in the butter until the mixture resembles coarse breadcrumbs. Stir in the egg yolks with just enough iced water to bind the mixture to a soft dough. Roll out on a lightly floured surface and line a deep 23 cm/9 in flan tin. Chill the pastry case for about 30 minutes.
2 Preheat oven to 190°C/375°F/Gas 5. Prick the pastry case all over with a fork, cover with greaseproof paper weighed down with baking beans and bake blind for 10 minutes. Remove the baking beans and paper, return the pastry case to the oven and bake for a further 10 minutes, until the pastry is crisp and golden. Cool in the tin.

POTS AU CHOCOLAT

The chocolate and chestnut mixture (minus the pastry) also makes delicious individual *pots au chocolat*. Make the fillings as described above; then simply pour the mixture into small ramekins that have been lightly greased with butter. Decorate with a blob of whipped cream and grated chocolate and serve with *langues de chat*.

CHOCOLATE AND CHESTNUT PIE

23 cm/9 in pastry case (see recipe
above), cooked

FOR THE FILLING

115g/4oz/½ cup butter, softened
115g/4oz/¼ cup caster sugar
425g/15oz can unsweetened chestnut
purée
225g/8oz plain chocolate, broken into
small pieces
30ml/2 tbsp brandy

1 Make the filling. Cream the butter with the caster sugar in a mixing bowl until pale and fluffy. Add the unsweetened chestnut purée, about 30ml/2 tbsp at a time, beating well after each addition.
2 Put the chocolate in a heatproof bowl. Place over a saucepan of barely simmering water until the chocolate has melted, stirring occasionally until smooth. Stir the chocolate into the chestnut mixture until combined, then add the brandy.
3 Pour the filling into the cold pastry case. Using a spatula, level the surface. Chill until set. Decorate with whipped cream and chocolate leaves, if desired, or simply add a dusting of sifted cocoa.

3 Make the filling. Mix the egg yolks, cornflour and 30ml/2 tbsp of the sugar in a bowl. Heat the milk in a saucepan until almost boiling, then beat into the egg mixture. Return to the clean pan and stir over a low heat until the custard has thickened and is smooth. Pour half the custard into a bowl.

4 Put the chocolate in a heatproof bowl. Place over a saucepan of barely simmering water until the chocolate has melted, stirring occasionally until smooth. Stir the melted chocolate into the custard in the bowl, with the vanilla essence. Spread the filling in the pastry case and cover closely with dampened greaseproof paper or clear film to prevent the formation of a skin. Allow to cool, then chill until set.

5 Sprinkle the gelatine over the water in a bowl, leave until spongy, then place the bowl over a pan of simmering water until all the gelatine has dissolved. Stir into the remaining custard, then add the rum. Whisk the egg whites in a clean, grease-free bowl until peaks form. Whisk in the remaining sugar, a little at a time, until stiff, then fold the egg whites quickly but evenly into the rum-flavoured custard.
6 Spoon the rum-flavoured custard over the chocolate layer in the pastry case. Using a spatula, level the mixture, making sure that none of the chocolate custard is visible. Return the pie to the fridge until the top layer has set, then remove the pie from the tin and place it on a serving plate. Whip the cream, spread it over the pie and sprinkle with chocolate curls, to decorate.

LUXURY WHITE CHOCOLATE CHEESECAKE

SERVES 16–20

150g / 5oz (about 16–18) digestive biscuits
50g / 2oz / ½ cup blanched hazelnuts, toasted
50g / 2oz / ¼ cup unsalted butter, melted
2.5ml / ½ tsp ground cinnamon
white chocolate curls, to decorate
cocoa powder, for dusting (optional)

FOR THE FILLING

350g / 12oz fine quality white chocolate,
chopped into small pieces
120ml / 4fl oz / ½ cup whipping cream or
double cream
675g / 1½lb / 3 x 8oz packets cream
cheese, softened
50g / 2oz / ¼ cup granulated sugar
4 eggs
30ml / 2 tbsp hazelnut-flavoured liqueur or
15ml / 1 tbsp vanilla essence

FOR THE TOPPING

450ml / ¾ pint / 1¾ cups soured cream
50g / 2oz / ¼ cup granulated sugar
15ml / 1 tbsp hazelnut-flavoured liqueur or
5ml / 1 tsp vanilla essence

3 Using a hand-held electric mixer, beat the cream cheese and sugar in a large bowl until smooth. Add the eggs one at a time, beating well. Slowly beat in the white chocolate mixture and liqueur or vanilla essence. Pour the filling into the baked crust. Place the tin on the hot baking sheet. Bake for 45–55 minutes, and do not allow the top to brown. Transfer the cheesecake to a wire rack while preparing the topping. Increase the oven temperature to 200°C/400°F/Gas 6.

4 Prepare the topping. In a small bowl whisk the soured cream, sugar and liqueur or vanilla essence until thoroughly mixed. Pour the mixture over the cheesecake, spreading it evenly, and return to the oven. Bake for a further 5–7 minutes. Turn off the oven, but do not open the door for 1 hour. Serve the cheesecake at room temperature, decorated with the white chocolate curls. Dust the surface lightly with cocoa powder, if desired.

1 Preheat oven to 180°C/350°F/Gas 4. Grease a 23 x 7.5 cm/9 x 3 in springform tin. In a food processor, process the biscuits and hazelnuts until fine crumbs form. Pour in the butter and cinnamon. Process just until blended. Using the back of a spoon, press on to the base and to within 1 cm/½ in of the top of the sides of the cake tin. Bake the crumb crust for 5–7 minutes, until just set. Cool in the tin on a wire rack. Lower the oven temperature to 150°C/300°F/Gas 2 and place a baking sheet inside to heat up.

2 Prepare the filling. In a small saucepan over a low heat, melt the white chocolate and cream until smooth, stirring frequently. Set aside to cool slightly.

CHOCOLATE TIRAMISU TART

SERVES 12–16

115g/4oz/½ cup unsalted butter
15ml/1 tbsp coffee-flavoured liqueur or water
175g/6oz/1½ cups plain flour
25g/1oz/¼ cup cocoa powder
25g/1oz/¼ cup icing sugar
pinch of salt
2.5ml/½ tsp vanilla essence
cocoa powder, for dusting

FOR THE CHOCOLATE LAYER
350ml/12fl oz/1½ cups double cream
15ml/1 tbsp golden syrup
115g/4oz bittersweet chocolate, chopped into small pieces
25g/1oz/2 tbsp unsalted butter, cut into small pieces
30ml/2 tbsp coffee-flavoured liqueur

FOR THE FILLING
250ml/8fl oz/1 cup whipping cream
350g/12oz/1½ cups mascarpone cheese, at room temperature
45ml/3 tbsp icing sugar
45ml/3 tbsp cold espresso or strong black coffee
45ml/3 tbsp coffee-flavoured liqueur
90g/3½oz plain chocolate, grated

1 Make the pastry. Lightly grease a 23 cm/9 in springform tin. In a saucepan, heat the butter and liqueur or water until the butter has melted. Sift the flour, cocoa, icing sugar and salt into a bowl. Remove the butter mixture from the heat, stir in the vanilla essence and gradually stir into the flour mixture until a soft dough forms.

2 Knead lightly until smooth. Press on to the base and up the sides of the tin to within 2 cm/¾ in of the top. Prick the dough. Chill for 40 minutes. Preheat oven to 190°C/375°F/Gas 5. Bake the pastry case for 8–10 minutes. If the pastry puffs up, prick it with a fork and bake for 2–3 minutes more until set. Cool in the tin on a rack.

3 Prepare the chocolate layer. Bring the cream and syrup to a boil in a pan over a medium heat. Off the heat, add the chocolate, stirring until melted. Beat in the butter and liqueur and pour into the pastry case. Cool completely, then chill.

4 Prepare the filling. Using a hand-held electric mixer, whip the cream in a bowl until soft peaks form. In another bowl, beat the cheese until soft, then beat in the icing sugar until smooth and creamy. Gradually beat in the cold coffee and liqueur; gently fold in the whipped cream and chocolate. Spoon the filling into the pastry case, on top of the chocolate layer. Level the surface. Chill until ready to serve.

5 To serve, run a sharp knife around the side of the tin to loosen the tart shell. Remove the side of the tin and slide the tart on to a plate. Sift a layer of cocoa powder over the tart to decorate, or pipe rosettes of whipped cream around the rim and top each with a chocolate-coated coffee bean. Chocolate Tiramisu Tart is very rich, so serve it in small wedges, with cups of espresso.

RASPBERRY, MASCARPONE AND WHITE CHOCOLATE CHEESECAKE

SERVES 8

50g/2oz/¼ cup unsalted butter
225g/8oz ginger biscuits, crushed
50g/2oz/½ cup chopped pecan nuts or walnuts

FOR THE FILLING

275g/10oz/1¼ cups mascarpone cheese
175g/6oz/¾ cup fromage frais
2 eggs, beaten
45ml/3 tbsp caster sugar
250g/9oz white chocolate, chopped into small pieces
225g/8oz/1½ cups fresh or frozen raspberries

FOR THE TOPPING

115g/4oz/½ cup mascarpone cheese
75g/3oz/⅓ cup fromage frais
white chocolate curls and fresh raspberries, to decorate

1 Preheat oven to 150°C/300°F/Gas 2. Melt the butter in a saucepan, then stir in the crushed biscuits and nuts. Press into the base of a 23 cm/9 in springform cake tin. Level the surface.

2 Make the filling. Using a wooden spoon, beat the mascarpone and fromage frais in a large mixing bowl, then beat in the eggs, a little at a time. Add the caster sugar. Beat until the sugar has dissolved, and the mixture is smooth and creamy.

3 Melt the white chocolate gently in a heatproof bowl over a saucepan of simmering water, then stir into the cheese mixture. Add the fresh or frozen raspberries and mix lightly.

4 Tip into the prepared tin and spread evenly, then bake for about 1 hour or until just set. Switch off the oven, but do not remove the cheesecake. Leave it until cold and completely set.

5 Remove the sides of the tin and carefully lift the cheesecake on to a serving plate. Make the topping by mixing the mascarpone and fromage frais in a bowl and spreading the mixture over the cheesecake. Decorate with chocolate curls and raspberries.

APRICOT AND WHITE CHOCOLATE CHEESECAKE

Use 225g/8oz/1 cup ready-to-eat dried apricots instead of the fresh or frozen raspberries in the cheesecake mixture. Slice the apricots thinly or dice them. Omit the mascarpone and fromage frais topping and serve the cheesecake with an apricot sauce, made by poaching 225g/8oz stoned fresh apricots in 120ml/4fl oz/½ cup water until tender, then rubbing the fruit and liquid through a sieve placed over a bowl. Sweeten the apricot purée with caster sugar to taste, and add enough lemon juice to sharpen the flavour. Alternatively, purée drained canned apricots with a little of their syrup, then stir in lemon juice to taste.

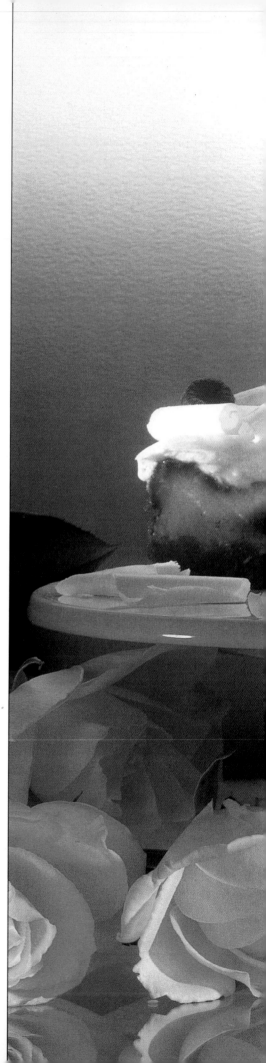

MISSISSIPPI MUD PIE

SERVES 8

175g/6oz/1½ cups plain flour
2.5ml/½ tsp salt
115g/4oz/½ cup butter
30–45ml/2–3 tbsp iced water

FOR THE FILLING

*75g/3oz plain chocolate, broken into
small pieces*
50g/2oz/¼ cup butter or margarine
45ml/3 tbsp golden syrup
3 eggs, beaten
*150g/5oz/⅔ cup soft light brown
sugar*
5ml/1 tsp vanilla essence

TO DECORATE

115g/4oz chocolate bar
300ml/½ pint/1¼ cups whipping cream

<u>1</u> Preheat oven to 220°C/425°F/Gas 7. Sift the flour and salt into a mixing bowl. Rub in the butter until the mixture resembles coarse breadcrumbs. Sprinkle in the water, about 15ml/1 tbsp at a time, and toss the mixture lightly with your fingers or a fork until the dough forms a ball.

<u>2</u> On a lightly floured surface, roll out the pastry and line a 23 cm/9 in flan tin, easing in the pastry and being careful not to stretch it. With your thumbs, make a fluted edge.

<u>3</u> Using a fork, prick the base and sides of the pastry case. Bake for 10–15 minutes, until lightly browned. Cool, in the pan.

<u>4</u> Make the filling. In a heatproof bowl set over a pan of barely simmering water, melt the plain chocolate with the butter or margarine and the golden syrup. Remove the bowl from the heat and stir in the eggs, sugar and vanilla essence.

<u>5</u> Lower the oven temperature to 180°C/350°F/Gas 4. Pour the chocolate mixture into the pastry case. Bake for 35–40 minutes, until the filling is set. Allow to cool completely in the flan tin, on a rack.

<u>6</u> Make the decoration. Use the heat of your hands to soften the chocolate bar slightly. Working over a sheet of non-stick baking paper, draw the blade of a swivel-bladed vegetable peeler across the side of the chocolate bar to shave off short, wide curls. Chill the curls until required.

<u>7</u> Before serving the pie, pour the cream into a bowl and whip to soft peaks. Spread over the top of the pie, hiding the chocolate filling completely. Decorate with the chocolate curls.

ITALIAN CHOCOLATE RICOTTA PIE

SERVES 6

225g / 8oz / 2 cups plain flour
30ml / 2 tbsp cocoa powder
60ml / 4 tbsp caster sugar
115g / 4oz / ½ cup unsalted butter
60ml / 4 tbsp dry sherry

FOR THE FILLING

2 egg yolks
115g / 4oz / ½ cup caster sugar
500g / 1¼lb / 2½ cups ricotta cheese
finely grated rind of 1 lemon
90ml / 6 tbsp dark chocolate chips
75ml / 5 tbsp chopped mixed peel
45ml / 3 tbsp chopped angelica

1 Sift the flour and cocoa into a bowl, then stir in the sugar. Rub in the butter using your fingertips, then work in the sherry to make a firm dough.

2 Preheat oven to 200°C / 400°F / Gas 6. Roll out three-quarters of the pastry on a lightly floured surface and line a 24 cm / 9½ in loose-based flan tin.

3 Make the filling. Beat the egg yolks and sugar in a bowl, then beat in the ricotta to mix thoroughly. Stir in the lemon rind, chocolate chips, mixed peel and angelica.

4 Scrape the ricotta mixture into the pastry case and level the surface. Roll out the remaining pastry and cut into strips. Arrange these in a lattice over the pie.
5 Bake for 15 minutes. Lower the oven temperature to 180°C / 350°F / Gas 4 and cook for a further 30–35 minutes, until golden brown and firm. Cool the pie in the tin. Serve at room temperature.

WHITE CHOCOLATE AND MANGO CREAM TART

SERVES 8

175g / 6oz / 1½ cups plain flour
75g / 3oz / 1 cup sweetened, desiccated coconut
115g / 4oz / ½ cup butter, softened
30ml / 2 tbsp caster sugar
2 egg yolks
2.5ml / ½ tsp almond essence
600ml / 1 pint / 2½ cups whipping cream
1 large ripe mango
*50g / 2oz / ½ cup toasted flaked almonds,
to decorate*

FOR THE WHITE CHOCOLATE
CUSTARD FILLING

*150g / 5oz fine quality white chocolate,
chopped into small pieces*
*120ml / 4fl oz / ½ cup whipping cream or
double cream*
75ml / 5 tbsp cornflour
15ml / 1 tbsp plain flour
50g / 2oz / ¼ cup granulated sugar
350ml / 12fl oz / 1½ cups milk
5 egg yolks

1 Using a hand-held electric mixer at low speed, beat the flour, coconut, butter, sugar, egg yolks and almond essence in a deep bowl until the mixture forms a soft dough. Lightly grease a 23 cm / 9 in tart tin with a removable base. Press the pastry on to the bottom and sides. Prick the pastry case with a fork. Chill the case for 30 minutes.

COOK'S TIP

Choose a mango that is a rich yellow in colour, with a pink or red blush. It should just yield to the touch, but should not be too soft. Peel it carefully, then cut it in half around the stone. Cut each piece in half again, then in neat slices.

2 Preheat oven to 180°C / 350°F / Gas 4. Line the pastry case with non-stick baking paper; fill with baking beans and bake blind for 10 minutes. Remove the paper and beans and bake for a further 5–7 minutes, until golden. Cool the cooked pastry in the tin on a wire rack.

3 Prepare the custard filling. In a small saucepan over a low heat, melt the white chocolate with the cream, stirring until smooth. Set aside. Combine the cornflour, plain flour and sugar in a medium saucepan. Stir in the milk gradually. Place over a medium heat and cook, stirring constantly, until the mixture has thickened.

4 Beat the egg yolks in a small bowl. Slowly add about 250ml / 8fl oz / 1 cup of the hot milk mixture, stirring constantly. Return the yolk mixture to the rest of the sauce in the pan, stirring constantly.

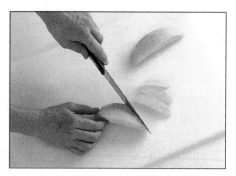

5 Bring the custard filling to a gentle boil, stirring constantly until thickened. Stir in the melted white chocolate until well blended. Cool to room temperature, stirring frequently to prevent a skin from forming on the surface. Beat the whipping cream in a medium-sized bowl until soft peaks form. Fold approximately 120ml / 4fl oz / ½ cup of the whipped cream into the white chocolate custard and spoon half the custard into the base. Peel and slice the mango thinly.

6 With the aid of a slim metal spatula or palette knife, arrange the mango slices over the custard in concentric circles, starting at the rim and then filling in the centre. Try to avoid moving the mango slices once in position. Carefully pour the remaining custard over the mango slices, smoothing the surface evenly. Remove the side of the tin and slide the tart carefully on to a serving plate.

7 Spoon the remaining flavoured cream into a large piping bag fitted with a medium star tip. Pipe the cream in a scroll pattern in parallel rows on top of the tart, keeping the rows about 1 cm / ½ in apart. Carefully sprinkle the toasted flaked almonds between the rows. Serve the tart chilled.

Hazelnut Chocolate Meringue Torte with Pears

Serves 8–10

175g / 6oz / ¾ cup granulated sugar
1 vanilla pod, split
475ml / 6fl oz / 2 cups water
4 ripe pears, peeled, halved and cored
*30ml / 2 tbsp hazelnut- or pear-flavoured
liqueur*
150g / 5oz / 1¼ cups hazelnuts, toasted
6 egg whites
pinch of salt
350g / 12oz / 2¼ cups icing sugar
5ml / 1 tsp vanilla essence
50g / 2oz plain chocolate, melted

For the Chocolate Cream

*275g / 10oz fine quality bittersweet or plain
chocolate, chopped into small pieces*
475ml / 16fl oz / 2 cups whipping cream
*60ml / 4 tbsp hazelnut- or pear-flavoured
liqueur*

1 In a saucepan large enough to hold the pears in a single layer combine the sugar, vanilla pod and water. Over a high heat, bring to the boil, stirring until the sugar dissolves. Lower the heat, add the pears to the syrup, cover and simmer gently for 12–15 minutes until tender. Remove the pan from the heat and allow the pears to cool in their poaching liquid. Carefully lift the pears out of the liquid and drain on kitchen paper. Transfer them to a plate, sprinkle with liqueur, cover and chill overnight.

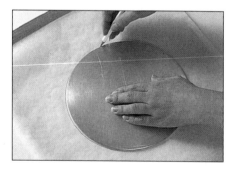

2 Preheat oven to 180°C/350°F/Gas 4. With a pencil draw a 23 cm/9 in circle on each of two sheets of non-stick baking paper. Turn the paper over on to two baking sheets (so that the pencil marks are underneath). Crumb the toasted hazelnuts in a food processor fitted with a metal blade.

3 In a large bowl, beat the whites with a hand-held electric mixer until frothy. Add the salt and beat on high speed until soft peaks form. Reduce the mixer speed and gradually add the icing sugar, beating well after each addition until all the sugar has been added and the whites are stiff and glossy; this will take 12–15 minutes. Gently fold in the nuts and vanilla essence and spoon the meringue on to the circles on the baking sheets, smoothing the top and sides.

4 Bake for 1 hour until the tops are dry and firm. Turn off the oven and allow to cool in the oven for 2–3 hours or overnight, until completely dry.

5 Prepare the chocolate cream. Melt the chocolate in a heatproof bowl set over a saucepan of simmering water. Stir the chocolate until melted and smooth. Cool to room temperature. Using a hand-held electric mixer beat the cream in a bowl to form soft peaks. Quickly fold the cream into the melted chocolate; fold in the liqueur. Spoon about one third of the chocolate cream into an icing bag fitted with a star tip. Set aside.

6 Thinly slice each pear half lengthwise with a sharp knife. Place one meringue layer on a serving plate. Spread with half the chocolate cream and arrange half the sliced pears evenly over the cream. Pipe a border of rosettes around the edge.

7 Top with the second meringue layer and spread with the remaining chocolate cream. Arrange the remaining pear slices in an attractive pattern over the chocolate cream. Pipe a border of rosettes around the edge. Spoon the melted chocolate into a small paper cone and drizzle the chocolate over the pears. Chill for at least 1 hour before serving.

CHOCOLATE, BANANA AND TOFFEE PIE

SERVES 6

65g / 2½oz / 5 tbsp unsalted butter,
melted
250g / 9oz milk chocolate digestive biscuits,
crushed
chocolate curls, to decorate

FOR THE FILLING

397g / 13oz can condensed milk
150g / 5oz plain chocolate, chopped
120ml / 4fl oz / ½ cup crème fraîche
15ml / 1 tbsp golden syrup

FOR THE TOPPING

2 bananas
250ml / 8fl oz / 1 cup crème fraîche
10ml / 2 tsp strong black coffee

1 Mix the butter with the biscuit crumbs. Press on to the base and sides of a 23cm/9in loose-based flan tin. Chill.

2 Make the filling. Place the unopened can of condensed milk in a deep saucepan of boiling water, making sure that it is completely covered. Lower the heat and simmer, covered for 2 hours, topping up the water as necessary. The can must remain covered at all times.

3 Remove the pan from the heat and set aside, covered, until the can has cooled down completely in the water. Do not attempt to open the can until it is completely cold.

4 Gently melt the chocolate with the crème fraîche and golden syrup in a heatproof bowl over a saucepan of simmering water. Stir in the caramelized condensed milk and beat until evenly mixed. Pour the filling into the biscuit crust and spread it evenly.

5 Slice the bananas evenly and arrange them over the chocolate filling.

6 Stir the crème fraîche and coffee together in a bowl, then spoon the mixture over the bananas. Sprinkle the chocolate curls on top. Alternatively, omit the crème fraîche topping and decorate with whipped cream and extra banana slices.

COLD DESSERTS

CHOCOLATE PROFITEROLES

4 Beat 1 egg in a small bowl and set aside. Add the whole eggs, one at a time, to the flour mixture, beating well after each addition. Beat in just enough of the beaten egg to make a smooth, shiny dough. It should pull away and fall slowly when dropped from a spoon.

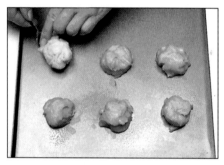

5 Using a tablespoon, ease the dough in 12 mounds on to the prepared baking sheet. Bake for 25–30 minutes, until the puffs are golden brown.

6 Remove the puffs from the oven and cut a small slit in the side of each of them to release the steam. Return the puffs to the oven, turn off the heat and leave them to dry out, with the oven door open.

7 Remove the ice cream from the freezer and allow it to soften for about 10 minutes. Split the profiteroles in half and put a small scoop of ice cream in each. Arrange on a serving platter or divide among individual plates. Pour the sauce over the profiteroles and serve at once.

SERVES 4-6
110g / 3¾oz / scant 1 cup plain flour
1.5ml / ¼ tsp salt
pinch of freshly grated nutmeg
175ml / 6fl oz / ¾ cup water
75g / 3oz / 6 tbsp unsalted butter, cut into
6 equal pieces
3 eggs
750ml / 1¼ pints / 3 cups vanilla ice cream
FOR THE CHOCOLATE SAUCE
275g / 10oz plain chocolate, chopped into
small pieces
120ml / 4fl oz / ½ cup warm water

1 Preheat oven to 200°C/400°F/Gas 6. Grease a baking sheet. Sift the flour, salt and nutmeg on to a sheet of greaseproof paper or foil.

2 Make the sauce. Melt the chocolate with the water in a heatproof bowl placed over a saucepan of barely simmering water. Stir until smooth. Keep warm until ready to serve, or reheat when required.

3 In a medium saucepan, bring the water and butter to the boil. Remove from the heat and add the dry ingredients all at once, funnelling them in from the paper or foil. Beat with a wooden spoon for about 1 minute until well blended and the mixture starts to pull away from the pan, then set the pan over a low heat and cook the mixture for about 2 minutes, beating constantly. Remove from the heat.

VARIATION
Fill the profiteroles with whipped cream, if you prefer. Spoon the cream into a piping bag and fill the slit puffs, or sandwich the halved puffs with the cream.

CHOCOLATE CONES WITH APRICOT SAUCE

SERVES 6

250g / 9oz plain dark chocolate, chopped into small pieces
350g / 12oz / 1½ cups ricotta cheese
45ml / 3 tbsp double cream
30ml / 2 tbsp brandy
30ml / 2 tbsp icing sugar
finely grated rind of 1 lemon
pared strips of lemon rind, to decorate

FOR THE SAUCE

175g / 6oz / ⅔ cup apricot jam
45ml / 3 tbsp lemon juice

<u>1</u> Cut twelve 10 cm/4 in double thickness rounds from non-stick baking paper and shape each into a cone. Secure with masking tape.

<u>2</u> Melt the chocolate over a saucepan of simmering water. Cool slightly, then spoon a little into each cone, swirling and brushing it to coat the paper evenly.

<u>3</u> Support each cone point downwards in a cup or glass held on its side, to keep it level. Leave in a cool place until the cones are completely set. Unless it is a very hot day, do not put the cones in the fridge, as this may mar their appearance.

<u>4</u> Make the sauce. Combine the apricot jam and lemon juice in a small saucepan. Melt over a gentle heat, stirring occasionally, then press through a sieve into a small bowl. Set aside to cool.

<u>5</u> Beat the ricotta cheese in a bowl until softened, then beat in the cream, brandy and icing sugar. Stir in the lemon rind. Spoon the mixture into a piping bag. Fill the cones, then carefully peel off the non-stick baking paper.

<u>6</u> Spoon a pool of apricot sauce on to six dessert plates. Arrange the cones in pairs on the plates. Decorate with a scattering of pared lemon rind strips and serve immediately.

CHOCOLATE HAZELNUT GALETTES

SERVES 4

175g/6oz plain chocolate, chopped into small pieces
45ml/3 tbsp single cream
30ml/2 tbsp flaked hazelnuts
115g/4oz white chocolate, chopped into small pieces
175g/6oz/¾ cup fromage frais (8% fat)
15ml/1 tbsp dry sherry
60ml/4 tbsp finely chopped hazelnuts, toasted physalis (Cape gooseberries), dipped in white chocolate, to decorate

1 Melt the plain chocolate in a heatproof bowl over a saucepan of barely simmering water, then remove the pan from the heat and lift off the bowl. Stir the cream into the melted chocolate. Draw twelve 7.5 cm/3 in circles on sheets of non-stick baking paper.

2 Turn the baking paper over and spread the plain chocolate over each marked circle, covering in a thin, even layer. Scatter flaked hazelnuts over four of the circles, then leave until set.

3 Melt the white chocolate in a heatproof bowl over hot water, then stir in the fromage frais and dry sherry. Fold in the chopped, toasted hazelnuts. Leave to cool until the mixture holds its shape.

4 Remove the plain chocolate rounds carefully from the paper and sandwich them together in stacks of three, spooning the white chocolate hazelnut cream between the layers and using the hazelnut-covered rounds on top. Chill before serving.

5 To serve, place the galettes on individual plates and decorate with chocolate-dipped physalis.

CHOCOLATE VANILLA TIMBALES

SERVES 6

350ml/12fl oz/1½ cups semi-skimmed milk
30ml/2 tbsp cocoa powder
2 eggs
10ml/2 tsp vanilla essence
45ml/3 tbsp granulated sweetener
15ml/1 tbsp/1 sachet powdered gelatine
45ml/3 tbsp hot water
extra cocoa powder, to decorate

FOR THE SAUCE

115g/4oz/½ cup light Greek-style yogurt
25ml/1½ tbsp vanilla essence

1 Place the milk and cocoa powder in a saucepan and stir until the milk is boiling. Separate the eggs and beat the egg yolks with the vanilla and sweetener in a bowl, until the mixture is pale and smooth. Gradually pour in the chocolate milk, beating well.

2 Return the mixture to the pan and stir constantly over a gentle heat, without boiling, until it is slightly thickened and smooth.

3 Remove the pan from the heat. Pour the gelatine into the hot water and stir until it is completely dissolved, then quickly stir it into the milk mixture. Put this mixture aside and allow it to cool until almost setting.

4 Whisk the egg whites until they hold soft peaks. Fold the egg whites quickly into the milk mixture. Spoon the timbale mixture into six individual moulds and chill them until set.

5 To serve, run a knife around the edge, dip the moulds quickly into hot water and turn out. Dust with cocoa. For the sauce, stir together the yogurt and vanilla and spoon on to the plates.

TIRAMISU IN CHOCOLATE CUPS

SERVES 6

1 egg yolk
30ml / 2 tbsp caster sugar
2.5ml / ½ tsp vanilla essence
250g / 9oz / generous 1 cup mascarpone cheese
120ml / 4fl oz / ½ cup strong black coffee
15ml / 1 tbsp cocoa powder
30ml / 2 tbsp coffee liqueur
16 amaretti biscuits
cocoa powder, for dusting

FOR THE CHOCOLATE CUPS

175g / 6oz plain chocolate, chopped
25g / 1oz / 2 tbsp unsalted butter

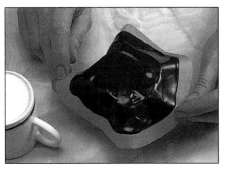

1 Make the chocolate cups. Cut out six 15 cm/6 in rounds of non-stick baking paper. Melt the chocolate with the butter in a heatproof bowl over a saucepan of simmering water. Stir until smooth, then spread a spoonful of the chocolate mixture over each circle, to within 2 cm/¾ in of the edge.

2 Carefully lift each paper round and drape it over an upturned teacup or ramekin so that the edges curve into frills. Leave until completely set, then carefully lift off and peel away the paper to reveal the chocolate cups.

3 Make the filling. Using a hand-held electric mixer, beat the egg yolk and sugar in a bowl until smooth, then stir in the vanilla essence. Soften the mascarpone if necessary, then stir it into the egg yolk mixture. Beat until smooth.

4 In a separate bowl, mix the coffee, cocoa and liqueur. Break up the biscuits roughly, then stir them into the mixture.

5 Place the chocolate cups on individual plates. Divide half the biscuit mixture among them, then spoon over half the mascarpone mixture.

6 Spoon over the remaining biscuit mixture (including any free liquid), top with the rest of the mascarpone mixture and dust lightly with cocoa powder. Chill for about 30 minutes before serving.

WHITE CHOCOLATE PARFAIT

SERVES 10

225g/8oz white chocolate, chopped into
small pieces
600ml/1 pint/ 2½ cups whipping cream
120ml/4fl oz/½ cup milk
10 egg yolks
15ml/1 tbsp caster sugar
40g/1½oz/½ cup desiccated coconut
120ml/4fl oz/½ cup canned sweetened
coconut milk
150g/5oz/1¼ cups unsalted macadamia nuts
curls of fresh coconut, to decorate

FOR THE CHOCOLATE ICING

225g/8oz plain chocolate, chopped into
small pieces
75g/3oz/6 tbsp butter
20ml/generous 1 tbsp golden syrup
175ml/6fl oz/¾ cup whipping cream

1 Carefully line the base and sides of a 1.4 litre/2⅓ pint/6 cup terrine mould or loaf tin with clear film.

2 Melt the chopped white chocolate with 50ml/2fl oz/¼ cup of the cream in the top of a double boiler or a heatproof bowl set over a saucepan of simmering water. Stir continually until the mixture is smooth. Set aside.

3 Put the milk in a pan. Add 250ml/ 8fl oz/1 cup of the remaining cream and bring to boiling point over a medium heat stirring constantly.

4 Meanwhile, whisk the egg yolks and caster sugar together in a large bowl, until thick and pale.

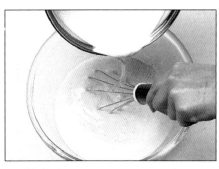

5 Add the hot cream mixture to the yolks, whisking constantly. Pour back into the saucepan and cook over a low heat for 2–3 minutes, until thickened. Stir constantly and do not boil. Remove the pan from the heat.

6 Add the melted chocolate, desiccated coconut and coconut milk, then stir well and leave to cool. Whip the remaining cream in a bowl until thick, then fold into the chocolate and coconut mixture.

7 Put 475ml/16fl oz/2 cups of the parfait mixture in the prepared mould or tin and spread evenly. Cover and freeze for about 2 hours, until just firm. Cover the remaining mixture and chill.

VARIATION

White Chocolate and Ginger Parfait: Use sliced stem ginger instead of macadamia nuts for the central layer of the parfait, and substitute syrup from the jar of ginger for the golden syrup in the icing. Leave out the coconut, if you prefer, and use sweetened condensed milk instead of the coconut milk.

8 Scatter the macadamia nuts evenly over the frozen parfait. Spoon in the remaining parfait mixture and level the surface. Cover the terrine and freeze for 6–8 hours or overnight, until the parfait is firm.

9 To make the icing, melt the chocolate with the butter and syrup in the top of a double boiler set over hot water. Stir occasionally.

10 Heat the cream in a saucepan, until just simmering, then stir into the chocolate mixture. Remove the pan from the heat and leave the mixture to cool until lukewarm.

11 To turn out the parfait, wrap the terrine or tin in a hot towel and set it upside down on a plate. Lift off the terrine or tin, then peel off the clear film. Place the parfait on a rack over a baking sheet and pour the icing evenly over the top. Working quickly, smooth the icing down the sides with a palette knife. Leave to set slightly, then transfer to a freezer-proof plate and freeze for 3–4 hours more.

12 Remove from the freezer about 15 minutes before serving, to allow the ice cream to soften slightly. When ready to serve, cut into slices, using a knife dipped in hot water between each slice. Serve, decorated with coconut curls.

CHOCOLATE AND CHESTNUT POTS

SERVES 6
250g/9oz plain chocolate
60ml/4 tbsp Madeira
25g/1oz/2 tbsp butter, diced
2 eggs, separated
225g/8oz/1 cup unsweetened chestnut purée
crème fraîche and chocolate curls, to decorate

1 Make a few chocolate curls for decoration, then break the rest of the chocolate into squares and melt it with the Madeira in a heatproof bowl over a saucepan of barely simmering water. Remove from the heat and add the butter, a few pieces at a time, stirring until melted and smooth.

2 Beat the egg yolks quickly into the mixture, then beat in the chestnut purée, a little at a time, making sure that each addition is absorbed before you add the next, mixing until smooth.

3 Whisk the egg whites in a clean, grease-free bowl until stiff. Stir about 15ml/1 tbsp of the whites into the chestnut mixture to lighten it, then fold in the rest evenly.

4 Spoon the mixture into six small ramekin dishes or custard cups and chill until set. Serve the pots topped with a generous spoonful of crème fraîche or whipped double cream. Decorate with the chocolate curls.

MOCHA VELVET CREAM POTS

SERVES 8
15ml/1 tbsp instant coffee powder
475ml/16fl oz/2 cups milk
75g/3oz/6 tbsp caster sugar
225g/8oz plain chocolate, chopped into small pieces
10ml/2 tsp vanilla essence
30ml/2 tbsp coffee liqueur (optional)
7 egg yolks
whipped cream and crystallized mimosa balls, to decorate

1 Preheat oven to 160°C/325°F/Gas 3. Place eight 120ml/4fl oz/½ cup custard cups or ramekins in a roasting tin. Set the tin aside.

2 Put the instant coffee into a saucepan. Stir in the milk, then add the sugar and set the pan over a medium heat. Bring to the boil, stirring constantly, until both the coffee and the sugar have dissolved completely.

3 Remove the pan from the heat and add the chocolate. Stir until it has melted and the sauce is smooth. Stir in the vanilla essence and coffee liqueur, if using.

4 In a bowl, whisk the egg yolks to blend them lightly. Slowly whisk in the chocolate mixture until well mixed, then strain the mixture into a large jug and divide equally among the cups or ramekins. Pour enough boiling water into the roasting tin to come halfway up the sides of the cups or ramekins. Carefully place the roasting tin in the oven.

5 Bake for 30–35 minutes, until the custard is just set and a knife inserted into the custard comes out clean. Remove the cups or ramekins from the roasting tin and allow to cool. Place on a baking sheet, cover and chill completely. Decorate with whipped cream and crystallized mimosa balls, if desired.

CHOCOLATE PAVLOVA WITH PASSION FRUIT CREAM

SERVES 6

4 egg whites
200g/7oz/scant 1 cup caster sugar
20ml/4 tsp cornflour
45ml/3 tbsp cocoa powder
5ml/1 tsp vinegar
chocolate leaves, to decorate

FOR THE FILLING

150g/5oz plain chocolate, chopped into
small pieces
250ml/8fl oz/1 cup double cream
150g/5oz/²⁄₃ cup Greek-style yogurt
2.5ml/½ tsp vanilla essence
4 passion fruit

1 Preheat oven to 140°C/275°F/Gas 1. Cut a piece of non-stick baking paper to fit a baking sheet. Draw a 23 cm/9 in circle on the paper.

2 Whisk the egg whites in a clean, grease-free bowl until stiff. Gradually whisk in the sugar and continue to whisk until the mixture is stiff again. Whisk in the cornflour, cocoa and vinegar.

3 Place the baking paper upside down on the baking sheet. Spread the mixture over the marked circle, making a slight dip in the centre. Bake for 1½–2 hours.

4 Make the filling. Melt the chocolate in a heatproof bowl over barely simmering water, then remove from the heat and cool slightly. In a separate bowl, whip the cream with the yogurt and vanilla essence until thick. Fold 60ml/4 tbsp into the chocolate, then set both mixtures aside.

5 Halve all the passion fruit and scoop out the pulp. Stir half into the plain cream mixture. Carefully remove the meringue shell from the baking sheet and place it on a large serving plate. Fill with the passion fruit cream, then spoon over the chocolate mixture and the remaining passion fruit pulp.

6 Decorate with chocolate leaves and serve as soon as possible, while the meringue is still crisp on the outside and deliciously chewy within.

Chocolate Sorbet

SERVES 6

150g / 5oz bittersweet chocolate, chopped
115g / 4oz plain chocolate, grated
225g / 8oz / 1¼ cups caster sugar
475ml / 16fl oz / 2 cups water
chocolate curls, to decorate

1 Put all the chocolate in a food processor, fitted with the metal blade, and process for 20–30 seconds until finely chopped.
2 In a saucepan over a medium heat, bring the sugar and water to the boil, stirring until the sugar dissolves. Boil for about 2 minutes, then remove the pan from the heat.
3 With the machine running, pour the hot syrup over the chocolate in the food processor. Keep the machine running for 1–2 minutes until the chocolate is completely melted and the mixture is smooth, scraping down the bowl once.
4 Strain the chocolate mixture into a large measuring jug or bowl. Leave to cool, then chill, stirring occasionally. Freeze the mixture in an ice-cream maker. Alternatively, pour into a container suitable for use in the freezer, freeze until slushy, whisk until smooth, then freeze again. Whisk for a second time before the mixture hardens completely. Allow the sorbet to soften for 5–10 minutes at room temperature and serve in scoops, decorated with chocolate curls.

Chocolate Sorbet with Red Fruits

SERVES 6

475ml / 16fl oz / 2 cups water
45ml / 3 tbsp clear honey
115g / 4oz / ½ cup caster sugar
75g / 3oz / ¾ cup cocoa powder
50g / 2oz plain dark or bittersweet chocolate, chopped into small pieces
400g / 14oz soft red fruits, such as raspberries, redcurrants or strawberries

1 Place the water, honey, caster sugar and cocoa powder in a saucepan. Heat gently, stirring occasionally, until the sugar has completely dissolved.
2 Remove the pan from the heat, add the chocolate and stir until melted. Leave until cool.
3 Tip into an ice-cream maker and churn until frozen. Alternatively, pour into a container suitable for use in the freezer, freeze until slushy, whisk until smooth, then freeze again. Whisk for a second time before the mixture hardens completely, and cover the container.
4 Remove from the freezer 10–15 minutes before serving, so that the sorbet softens slightly. Serve in scoops in chilled dessert bowls, with the soft fruits.

CHOCOLATE MINT ICE CREAM PIE

SERVES 8

75g / 3 oz plain chocolate chips
40g / 1½oz butter or margarine
50g / 2oz crisped rice cereal
1 litre / 1¾ pints / 4 cups mint-chocolate-chip
ice cream
chocolate curls, to decorate

<u>1</u> Line a 23 cm/9 in pie tin with foil. Place a round of greaseproof paper over the foil in the bottom of the tin.
<u>2</u> In a heatproof bowl set over a saucepan of simmering water melt the chocolate chips with the butter or margarine.
<u>3</u> Remove the bowl from the heat and gently stir in the cereal, a little at a time.

<u>4</u> Press the chocolate-cereal mixture evenly over the base and up the sides of the prepared tin, forming a 1 cm/½ in rim. Chill until completely hard.
<u>5</u> Carefully remove the cereal base from the tin and peel off the foil and paper. Return the base to the pie tin.

<u>6</u> Remove the ice cream from the freezer and allow it to soften for 10 minutes.

<u>7</u> Spread the ice cream evenly in the biscuit case crust. Freeze until firm.
<u>8</u> Scatter the chocolate curls over the ice cream just before serving.

Ice Cream Bombes

Serves 6

*1 litre / 1¾ pints / 4 cups soft-scoop chocolate
ice cream*
*475ml / 16fl oz / 2 cups soft-scoop vanilla
ice cream*
50g / 2oz / ⅓ cup plain chocolate chips
115g / 4oz toffees
75ml / 5 tbsp double cream

<u>1</u> Divide the chocolate ice cream equally among six small cups. Push it roughly to the base and up the sides, leaving a small cup-shaped dip in the middle. Return to the freezer and leave for 45 minutes. Take the cups out again and smooth the ice cream in each into shape, keeping the centre hollow. Return to the freezer.

<u>2</u> Put the vanilla ice cream in a small bowl and break it up slightly with a spoon. Stir in the chocolate chips and use this mixture to fill the hollows in the cups of chocolate ice cream. Smooth the tops, then cover the cups with clear film, return to the freezer and leave overnight.

<u>3</u> Melt the toffees with the cream in a small pan over a very low heat, stirring constantly until smooth, warm and creamy.

<u>4</u> Turn out the bombes on to individual plates and pour the toffee sauce over the top. Serve immediately.

CHOCOLATE FUDGE SUNDAES

SERVES 4

4 scoops each vanilla and coffee ice cream
2 small ripe bananas
whipped cream
toasted flaked almonds

FOR THE SAUCE

50g / 2oz / ⅓ cup soft light brown sugar
120ml / 4fl oz / ½ cup golden syrup
45ml / 3 tbsp strong black coffee
5ml / 1 tsp ground cinnamon
150g / 5oz plain chocolate, chopped into small pieces
75ml / 3fl oz / 5 tbsp whipping cream
45ml / 3 tbsp coffee-flavoured liqueur (optional)

1 Make the sauce. Place the sugar, syrup, coffee and cinnamon in a heavy-based saucepan. Bring to the boil, then boil for about 5 minutes, stirring the mixture constantly.

2 Turn off the heat and stir in the chocolate. When the chocolate has melted and the mixture is smooth, stir in the cream and the liqueur, if using. Leave the sauce to cool slightly. If made ahead, reheat the sauce gently until just warm.

3 Fill four glasses with a scoop each of vanilla and coffee ice cream.

4 Peel the bananas and slice them thinly. Scatter the sliced bananas over the ice cream. Pour the warm fudge sauce over the bananas, then top each sundae with a generous swirl of whipped cream. Sprinkle the sundaes with toasted almonds and serve at once.

CHOCOLATE ICE CREAM

SERVES 4–6

750ml/1¼ pints/3 cups milk
10 cm/4 in piece of vanilla pod
4 egg yolks
115g/4oz/½ cup granulated sugar
225g/8oz plain chocolate, chopped into
small pieces

1 Heat the milk with the vanilla pod in a small saucepan. Remove from the heat as soon as small bubbles start to form on the surface. Do not let it boil. Strain the milk into a jug and set aside.

2 Using a wire whisk or hand-held electric mixer, beat the egg yolks in a bowl. Gradually whisk in the sugar and continue to whisk until the mixture is pale and thick. Slowly add the milk to the egg mixture, whisking after each addition. When all the milk has been added, pour the mixture into a heatproof bowl.

3 Place the heatproof bowl over a saucepan of simmering water and add the chocolate. Stir over a low heat until the chocolate melts, then raise the heat slightly and continue to stir the chocolate-flavoured custard until it thickens enough to coat the back of a wooden spoon lightly. Remove the custard from the heat, pour into a bowl and allow to cool, stirring occasionally to prevent skin forming on the surface.

4 Freeze the chocolate mixture in an ice-cream maker, following the manufacturer's instructions, or pour it into a suitable container for freezing. Freeze for about 3 hours, or until set. Remove from the container and chop roughly into 7.5 cm/3 in pieces. Place in a food processor and chop until smooth. Return to the freezer container and freeze again. Repeat two or three times, until the ice cream is smooth and creamy.

ROCKY ROAD ICE CREAM

SERVES 6

*115g/4oz plain chocolate, chopped into
small pieces
150ml/¼ pint/⅔ cup milk
300ml/½ pint/1¼ cups double cream
115g/4oz/2 cups marshmallows, chopped
115g/4oz/½ cup glacé cherries, chopped
50g/2oz/½ cup crumbled shortbread biscuits
30ml/2 tbsp chopped walnuts*

1 Melt the chocolate in the milk in a saucepan over a gentle heat, stirring from time to time. Pour into a bowl and leave to cool completely.

2 Whip the cream in a separate bowl until it just holds its shape. Beat in the chocolate mixture, a little at a time, until the mixture is smooth and creamy.

3 Tip the mixture into an ice-cream maker and, following the manufacturer's instructions, churn until almost frozen. Alternatively, pour into a container suitable for use in the freezer, freeze until ice crystals form around the edges, then whisk with a strong hand whisk or hand-held electric mixer until smooth.

4 Stir the marshmallows, glacé cherries, crushed biscuits and nuts into the iced mixture, then return to the freezer container and freeze until firm.

5 Allow the ice cream to soften at room temperature for 15–20 minutes before serving in scoops. Add a wafer and chocolate sauce to each portion, if desired.

LITTLE CAKES,
BISCUITS & BARS

CHUNKY CHOCOLATE BARS

MAKES 12

*350g/12oz plain chocolate, chopped into
small pieces
115g/4oz/½ cup unsalted butter
400g/14oz can condensed milk
225g/8oz digestive biscuits, broken
50g/2oz/⅓ cup raisins
115g/4oz ready-to-eat dried peaches,
roughly chopped
50g/2oz/½ cup hazelnuts or pecan nuts,
roughly chopped*

1 Line a 28 x 18 cm/11 x 7 in cake tin
with clear film.

2 Melt the chocolate and butter in a large
heatproof bowl over a pan of simmering
water. Stir until well mixed.

3 Pour the condensed milk into the
chocolate and butter mixture. Beat with a
wooden spoon until creamy.

4 Add the broken biscuits, raisins,
chopped peaches and hazelnuts or pecans.
Mix well until all the ingredients are
coated in the rich chocolate sauce.

5 Tip the mixture into the prepared tin,
making sure it is pressed well into the
corners. Leave the top craggy. Cool, then
chill until set.

6 Lift the cake out of the tin using the
clear film and then peel off the film. Cut
into 12 bars and serve at once.

CHOCOLATE LEMON TARTLETS

MAKES 12 TARTLETS

450g/1lb Shortcrust Pastry
lemon twists and melted chocolate to decorate
FOR THE LEMON CUSTARD SAUCE
grated rind and juice of 1 lemon
350ml/12fl oz/1½ cups milk
6 egg yolks
50g/2oz/½ cup caster sugar
FOR THE LEMON CURD FILLING
grated rind and juice of 2 lemons
175g/6oz/¾ cup unsalted butter, diced
450g/1lb/2 cups granulated sugar
3 eggs, lightly beaten
FOR THE CHOCOLATE LAYER
175ml/6fl oz/¾ cup double cream
175g/6oz bittersweet or plain chocolate,
chopped into small pieces
25g/1oz/2 tbsp unsalted butter, cut into
pieces

1 Prepare the custard sauce. Place the rind in a saucepan with the milk. Bring to the boil over a medium heat. Remove from the heat and allow to stand for 5 minutes to infuse. Strain the milk into a clean pan and reheat it gently.

2 In a bowl beat the yolks and sugar with a hand-held electric mixer for 2–3 minutes, until pale and thick. Pour over about 250ml/8fl oz/1 cup of the flavoured hot milk, beating vigorously.

3 Return the yolk mixture to the rest of the milk in the pan and cook gently, stirring constantly, over low heat until the mixture thickens and lightly coats the back of a spoon. (Do not allow sauce to boil or it will curdle.) Strain into a chilled bowl. Stir 30ml/2 tbsp lemon juice into the sauce. Cool, stirring occasionally, then chill until ready to use.

4 Prepare the lemon curd filling. Combine the lemon rind, juice, butter and sugar in the top of a double boiler. Set over simmering water and heat gently until the butter has melted and the sugar has completely dissolved. Reduce the heat to low.

5 Stir the lightly beaten eggs into the butter mixture. Cook over a low heat, for 15 minutes, stirring constantly, until the mixture coats the back of a spoon.

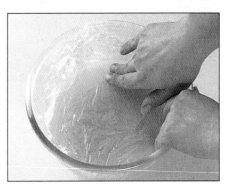

6 Strain the lemon curd into a bowl and cover closely with clear film. Allow to cool, stirring occasionally, then chill to thicken, stirring occasionally.

7 Lightly butter twelve 7.5 cm/3 in tartlet tins (if possible ones which have removable bases). On a lightly floured surface, roll out the pastry to a thickness of 3 mm/⅛ in. Using a 10 cm/4 in fluted cutter, cut out 12 rounds and press each one into a tartlet tin. Prick the bases with a fork. Place the tins on a baking sheet and chill for 30 minutes.

8 Preheat oven to 190°C/375°F/Gas 5. Cut out rounds of foil and line each pastry case; fill with baking beans or rice. Bake blind for 5–8 minutes. Remove the foil with the beans and bake for 5 more minutes, until the cases are golden. Remove to rack to cool.

9 Prepare the chocolate layer. In a saucepan over a medium heat, bring the cream to the boil. Remove from the heat and add the chocolate all at once; stir until melted. Beat in the butter and cool slightly. Pour the filling into each tartlet to make a layer 5 mm/¼ in thick. Chill for 10 minutes until set.

10 Remove the tartlets from the tins and spoon in a layer of lemon curd to come to the top of the pastry. Set aside, but do not chill. To serve, spoon a little lemon custard sauce on to a plate and place a tartlet in the centre. Decorate with a lemon twist. Dot the custard with melted chocolate. Draw a skewer through the chocolate to make heart motifs.

CHOCOLATE-DIPPED HAZELNUT CRESCENTS

MAKES ABOUT 35

275g/10oz/2 cups plain flour
pinch of salt
225g/8oz/1 cup unsalted butter, softened
75g/3oz/6 tbsp caster sugar
15ml/1 tbsp hazelnut-flavoured liqueur
or water
5ml/1 tsp vanilla essence
75g/3oz plain chocolate, chopped into
small pieces
50g/2oz/½ cup hazelnuts, toasted and
finely chopped
icing sugar, for dusting
350g/12oz plain chocolate, melted, for
dipping

1 Preheat oven to 160°C/325°F/Gas 3. Grease two large baking sheets. Sift the flour and salt into a bowl. In a separate bowl, beat the butter until creamy. Add the sugar and beat until fluffy, then beat in the hazelnut liqueur or water and the vanilla essence. Gently stir in the flour mixture, then the chocolate and hazelnuts.
2 With floured hands, shape the dough into 5 x 1 cm/2 x ½ in crescent shapes. Place on the baking sheets, 5 cm/2 in apart. Bake for 20–25 minutes until the edges are set and the biscuits slightly golden. Remove the biscuits from the oven and cool on the baking sheets for 10 minutes, then transfer the biscuits to wire racks to cool completely.

3 Have the melted chocolate ready in a small bowl. Dust the biscuits lightly with icing sugar. Using a pair of kitchen tongs or your fingers, dip half of each crescent into the melted chocolate. Place the crescents on a non-stick baking sheet until the chocolate has set.

BRIOCHES AU CHOCOLAT

MAKES 12

250g / 9oz / 2¼ cups strong white flour
pinch of salt
30ml / 2 tbsp caster sugar
1 sachet easy-blend dried yeast
3 eggs, beaten, plus extra beaten egg,
for glazing
45ml / 3 tbsp hand-hot milk
115g / 4oz / ½ cup unsalted butter, diced
175g / 6oz plain chocolate, broken into
squares

1 Sift the flour and salt into a large mixing bowl and stir in the sugar and yeast. Make a well in the centre of the mixture and add the eggs and milk.

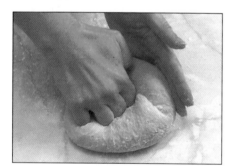

2 Beat the egg and milk mixture well, gradually incorporating the surrounding dry ingredients to make a fairly soft dough. Turn the dough on to a lightly floured surface and knead well for about 5 minutes, until smooth and elastic, adding a little more flour if necessary.
3 Add the butter to the dough, a few pieces at a time, kneading until each addition is absorbed before adding the next. When all the butter has been incorporated and small bubbles appear in the dough, wrap it in clear film and chill for at least 1 hour. If you intend serving the brioches for breakfast, the dough can be left overnight.

4 Lightly grease 12 individual brioche tins set on a baking sheet or a 12-hole brioche or patty tin. Divide the brioche dough into 12 pieces and shape each into a smooth round. Place a chocolate square in the centre of each round. Bring up the sides of the dough and press the edges firmly together to seal, use a little beaten egg if necessary.
5 Place the brioches, join side down, in the prepared tins. Cover and leave them in a warm place for about 30 minutes or until doubled in size. Preheat oven to 200°C/400°F/Gas 6.

6 Brush the brioches with beaten egg. Bake for 12–15 minutes, until well risen and golden brown. Place on wire racks and leave until they have cooled slightly. They should be served warm and can be made in advance and reheated if necessary. Do not serve straight from the oven, as the chocolate will be very hot.

COOK'S TIP
Brioches freeze well for up to 1 month. Thaw at room temperature, then reheat on baking sheets in a low oven and serve warm, but not hot. For a richer variation serve with melted chocolate drizzled over the top of the brioches.

CHOCOLATE AND TOFFEE BARS

MAKES 32

350g / 12oz / 2 cups soft light brown sugar
450g / 1lb / 2 cups butter or margarine, at room temperature
2 egg yolks
7.5ml / 1½ tsp vanilla essence
450g / 1lb / 4 cups plain or wholemeal flour
2.5ml / ½ tsp salt
175g / 6oz plain chocolate, broken into squares
115g / 4oz / 1 cup walnuts or pecan nuts, chopped

1 Preheat oven to 180°C / 350°F / Gas 4. Beat the sugar and
butter or margarine in a mixing bowl until light and fluffy. Beat
in the egg yolks and vanilla essence, then stir in the flour and salt
to make a soft dough.

2 Spread the dough in a greased 33 x 23 x 5 cm / 13 x 9 x 2 in
baking tin. Level the surface. Bake for 25–30 minutes, until
lightly browned. The texture will be soft.

3 Remove the bake from the oven and immediately place the
chocolate on top. Set aside until the chocolate is soft, then
spread it out with a spatula. Sprinkle with the chopped nuts.

4 While the bake is still warm, cut it into 5 x 4 cm / 2 x 1½ in
bars, remove from the tin and leave to cool on a wire rack.

CHOCOLATE PECAN SQUARES

MAKES 16

2 eggs
10ml / 2 tsp vanilla essence
pinch of salt
175g / 6oz / 1½ cups pecan nuts, roughly chopped
50g / 2oz / ½ cup plain flour
50g / 2oz / ¼ cup granulated sugar
120ml / 4fl oz / ½ cup golden syrup
75g / 3oz plain chocolate, chopped into small pieces
40g / 1½oz / 3 tbsp unsalted butter
16 pecan nut halves, to decorate

1 Preheat oven to 160°C / 325°F / Gas 3. Line a 20 cm / 8 in
square baking tin with non-stick baking paper.

2 In a bowl, whisk the eggs with the vanilla essence and salt. In
another bowl, mix together the pecan nuts and flour.

3 Put the sugar in a saucepan, add the golden syrup and bring to
the boil. Remove from the heat and stir in the chocolate and
butter with a wooden spoon until both have dissolved and the
mixture is smooth. Stir in the beaten egg mixture, then fold in
the pecan nuts and flour.

4 Pour the mixture into the prepared tin and bake for about 35
minutes or until firm to the touch. Cool in the tin for 10
minutes before turning out on a wire rack. Cut into 5 cm / 2 in
squares and press pecan halves into the tops while still warm.
Cool completely before serving.

WHITE CHOCOLATE BROWNIES WITH MILK CHOCOLATE MACADAMIA TOPPING

SERVES 12

115g/4oz/1 cup plain flour
2.5ml/½ tsp baking powder
pinch of salt
*175g/6oz fine quality white chocolate,
chopped into small pieces*
115g/4oz/½ cup caster sugar
*115g/4oz/½ cup unsalted butter, cut into
small pieces*
2 eggs, lightly beaten
5ml/1 tsp vanilla essence
*175g/6oz plain chocolate chips or plain
chocolate, chopped into small pieces*

FOR THE TOPPING

*200g/7oz milk chocolate, chopped into
small pieces*
*175g/6oz/1½ cups unsalted macadamia
nuts, chopped*

1 Preheat oven to 180°C/350°F/Gas 4. Grease a 23 cm/9 in springform tin. Sift together the flour, baking powder and salt, set aside.

2 In a medium saucepan over a low heat, melt the white chocolate, sugar and butter until smooth, stirring frequently. Cool slightly, then beat in the eggs and vanilla essence. Stir in the flour mixture until well blended. Stir in the chocolate chips or chopped chocolate. Spread evenly in the prepared tin.

3 Bake for 20–25 minutes, until a cake tester inserted in the cake tin comes out clean; do not over-bake. Remove the cake from the oven and place the tin on a heatproof surface.

4 Sprinkle the chopped milk chocolate evenly over the cake and return it to the oven for 1 minute.

5 Remove the cake from the oven again and gently spread the softened chocolate evenly over the top. Sprinkle with the macadamia nuts and gently press them into the chocolate. Cool on a wire rack for 30 minutes, then chill, for about 1 hour, until set. Run a sharp knife around the side of the tin to loosen, then unclip the side of the springform tin and remove it carefully. Cut into thin wedges.

CHUNKY DOUBLE CHOCOLATE COOKIES

MAKES 18–20

115g/4oz/½ cup unsalted butter, softened
115g/4oz/⅔ cup light muscovado sugar
1 egg
5ml/1 tsp vanilla essence
150g/5oz/1¼ cups self-raising flour
75g/3oz/¾ cup porridge oats
115g/4oz plain chocolate, roughly chopped
115g/4oz white chocolate, roughly chopped

DOUBLE-CHOC ALMOND COOKIES:
Instead of the porridge oats, use
75g/3oz/¾ cup ground almonds.
Omit the chopped chocolate and use
175g/6oz/1 cup chocolate chips
instead. Top each heap of cake
mixture with half a glacé cherry
before baking.

1 Preheat oven to 190°C/375°F/Gas 5.
Lightly grease two baking sheets. Cream
the butter with the sugar in a bowl until
pale and fluffy. Add the egg and vanilla
essence and beat well.

2 Sift the flour over the mixture and fold
in lightly with a metal spoon, then add
the oats and chopped plain and white
chocolate and stir until evenly mixed.

3 Place small spoonfuls of the mixture in
18–20 rocky heaps on the baking sheets,
leaving space for spreading.

4 Bake for 12–15 minutes or until the
biscuits are beginning to turn pale
golden. Cool for 2–3 minutes on the
baking sheets, then lift on to wire racks.
The biscuits will be soft when freshly
baked but will harden on cooling.

CHOCOLATE KISSES

MAKES 24

75g / 3oz dark plain chocolate, chopped into
small pieces
75g / 3oz white chocolate, chopped into small
pieces
115g / 4oz / ½ cup butter, softened
115g / 4oz / ½ cup caster sugar
2 eggs
225g / 8oz / 2 cups plain flour
icing sugar, to decorate

1 Melt the plain and white chocolates in separate bowls and set both aside to cool.
2 Beat the butter and caster sugar together until pale and fluffy. Beat in the eggs, one at a time. Then sift in the flour and mix well.

3 Halve the creamed mixture and divide it between the two bowls of chocolate. Mix each chocolate in thoroughly so that each forms a dough. Knead the doughs until smooth, wrap them separately in clear film and chill for 1 hour. Preheat oven to 190°C / 375°F / Gas 5.

4 Shape slightly rounded teaspoonfuls of both doughs roughly into balls. Roll the balls between your palms to neaten them. Arrange the balls on greased baking sheets and bake for 10–12 minutes. Dust liberally with sifted icing sugar and cool on a wire rack.

CHOCOLATE CINNAMON TUILES

3 In a separate bowl, mix together the cocoa and cinnamon. Stir into the larger quantity of mixture until well combined. Leaving room for spreading, drop spoonfuls of the chocolate-flavoured mixture on to the prepared baking sheets, then spread each gently with a palette knife to make a neat round.

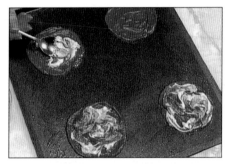

4 Using a small spoon, drizzle the reserved plain mixture over the rounds, swirling it lightly to give a marbled effect.

5 Bake for 4–6 minutes, until just set. Using a palette knife, lift each biscuit and drape it over a rolling pin, to give a curved shape as it hardens. Allow the tuiles to set, then remove them and finish cooling on a wire rack. Serve on the same day.

CHOCOLATE CUPS

Cream 150g/5oz/⅔ cup butter with 115g/4oz/½ cup caster sugar. Stir in 75g/3oz/1 cup porridge oats, 15ml/1 tbsp cocoa powder and 5ml/1 tsp vanilla essence. Roll to the size of golf balls and space well on greased baking sheets. Bake at 180°C/350°F/Gas 4 for 12–15 minutes. Cool slightly then drape over greased upturned glasses until cool and firm. Makes 8–10.

MAKES 12

1 egg white
50g/2oz/¼ cup caster sugar
30ml/2 tbsp plain flour
40g/1½oz/3 tbsp butter, melted
15ml/1 tbsp cocoa powder
2.5m/½ tsp ground cinnamon

1 Preheat oven to 200°C/400°F/Gas 6. Lightly grease two large baking sheets. Whisk the egg white in a clean, grease-free bowl until it forms soft peaks. Gradually whisk in the sugar to make a smooth, glossy mixture.

2 Sift the flour over the meringue mixture and fold in evenly; try not to deflate the mixture. Stir in the butter. Transfer about 45ml/3 tbsp of the mixture to a small bowl and set it aside.

CHOCOLATE MARZIPAN COOKIES

MAKES ABOUT 36

*200g / 7oz / scant 1 cup unsalted butter,
softened*
*200g / 7oz / generous 1 cup light muscovado
sugar*
1 egg, beaten
300g / 11oz / 2¾ cups plain flour
60ml / 4 tbsp cocoa powder
200g / 7oz white almond paste
*115g / 4oz white chocolate, chopped into
small pieces*

1 Preheat oven to 190°C/375°F/Gas 5. Lightly grease two large baking sheets. Using a hand-held electric mixer, cream the butter with the sugar in a mixing bowl until pale and fluffy. Add the egg and beat well.

2 Sift the flour and cocoa over the mixture. Stir in with a wooden spoon until all the flour mixture has been smoothly incorporated, then use clean hands to press the mixture together to make a fairly soft dough.

3 Using a rolling pin and keeping your touch light, roll out about half the dough on a lightly floured surface to a thickness of about 5 mm / ¼ in. Using a 5 cm / 2 in plain or fluted biscuit cutter, cut out 36 rounds, re-rolling the dough as required. Wrap the remaining dough in clear film and set it aside.

4 Cut the almond paste into 36 equal pieces. Roll into balls, flatten slightly and place one on each round of dough. Roll out the remaining dough, cut out more rounds, then place on top of the almond paste. Press the dough edges to seal.

5 Bake for 10–12 minutes, or until the cookies have risen well and are beginning to crack on the surface. Cool on the baking sheet for about 2–3 minutes, then finish cooling on a wire rack.

6 Melt the white chocolate, then either drizzle it over the biscuits to decorate, or spoon into a paper piping bag and quickly pipe a design on to the biscuits.

VARIATION
Use glacé icing instead of melted white chocolate to decorate the cookies, if you prefer.

SWEETS & TRUFFLES

DOUBLE CHOCOLATE-DIPPED FRUIT

MAKES 24 COATED PIECES

fruits – about 24 pieces (strawberries, cherries, orange segments, large seedless grapes, physalis (Cape gooseberries), kumquats, stoned prunes, stoned dates, dried apricots, dried peaches or dried pears)
115g/4oz white chocolate, chopped into small pieces
115g/4oz bittersweet or plain chocolate, chopped into small pieces

1 Clean and prepare fruits; wipe strawberries with a soft cloth or brush gently with pastry brush. Wash firm-skinned fruits such as cherries and grapes and dry well. Peel and leave whole or cut up any other fruits being used.

CHOCOLATE PEPPERMINT CREAMS

1 egg white
90ml/6 tbsp double cream
5ml/1 tsp peppermint essence
675g/1½lb/5½ cups icing sugar, plus extra for dusting
few drops of green food colouring
175g/6oz plain chocolate, chopped into small pieces

1 Beat the egg white lightly in a bowl. Mix in the cream and peppermint essence, then gradually add the icing sugar to make a firm, pliable dough. Work in 1–2 drops of green food colouring (apply it from a cocktail stick if you are anxious about adding too much colour) until the dough is an even, pale green.
2 On a surface dusted with icing sugar, roll out the dough to a thickness of about 1cm/½in. Stamp out 4cm/1½in rounds of squares and place on a baking sheet lined with non-stick baking paper. Leave to dry for at least 8 hours, turning once.
3 Melt the chocolate in a bowl over barely simmering water. Allow to cool slightly. Spread chocolate over the top of each peppermint cream, and place them on fresh sheets of non-stick paper. Chill until set.

2 Melt the white chocolate. Remove from the heat and cool to tepid (about 29°C/84°F), stirring frequently. Line a baking sheet with non-stick baking paper. Holding each fruit by the stem or end and at an angle, dip about two-thirds of the fruit into the chocolate. Allow the excess to drip off and place on the baking sheet. Chill the fruits for about 20 minutes until the chocolate sets.

3 Melt the bittersweet or plain chocolate, stirring frequently until smooth.

4 Remove the chocolate from the heat and cool to just below body temperature, about 30°C/86°F. Take each white chocolate-coated fruit in turn from the baking sheet and, holding by the stem or end and at the opposite angle, dip the bottom third of each piece into the dark chocolate, creating a chevron effect. Set on the baking sheet. Chill for 15 minutes or until set. Before serving, allow the fruit to stand at room temperature 10–15 minutes before serving.

Rich Chocolate Pistachio Fudge

Makes 36

250g/9oz/generous 1 cup granulated sugar
375g/13oz can sweetened condensed milk
50g/2oz/¼ cup unsalted butter
5ml/1 tsp vanilla essence
115g/4oz plain dark chocolate, grated
75g/3oz/¾ cup pistachio nuts, almonds or hazelnuts

CHOCOLATE-AND-MARSHMALLOW FUDGE

25g/1oz/2 tbsp butter
350g/12oz/1½ cups granulated sugar
175ml/6fl oz/¾ cup evaporated milk
pinch of salt
115g/4oz/2 cups white mini marshmallows
225g/8oz/1¼ cups chocolate chips
5ml/1 tsp vanilla essence
115g/4oz/1½ cup chopped walnuts (optional)

1 Generously grease an 18cm/7 in cake tin. Mix the butter, sugar, evaporated milk and salt in a heavy-based saucepan. Stir over a medium heat until the sugar has dissolved, then bring to the boil and cook for 3–5 minutes or until thickened, stirring all the time.

2 Remove the pan from the heat and beat in the marshmallows and chocolate chips until dissolved. Beat in the vanilla essence. Scrape the mixture into the prepared cake tin and press it evenly into the corners, using a metal palette knife. Level the surface.

3 If using the walnuts, sprinkle them over the fudge and press them in to the surface. Set the fudge aside to cool. Before it has set completely, mark it into squares with a sharp knife. Chill until firm before cutting the fudge up and serving it.

1 Grease a 19cm/7½in square cake tin and line with non-stick baking paper. Mix the sugar, condensed milk and butter in a heavy-based pan. Heat gently, stirring occasionally, until the sugar has dissolved completely and the mixture is smooth.

2 Bring the mixture to the boil, stirring occasionally, and boil until it registers 116°C/240°F on a sugar thermometer or until a small amount of the mixture dropped into a cup of iced water forms a soft ball.

3 Remove the pan from the heat and beat in the vanilla essence, chocolate and nuts. Beat vigorously until the mixture is smooth and creamy.

4 Pour the mixture into the prepared cake tin and spread evenly. Leave until just set, then mark into squares. Leave to set completely before cutting into squares and removing from the tin. Store in an airtight container in a cool place.

Chocolate-coated Nut Brittle

Makes 20–24 pieces

*115g/4oz/1 cup mixed pecan nuts and whole
almonds*
115g/4oz/½ cup caster sugar
60ml/4 tbsp water
*200g/7oz plain dark chocolate, chopped into
small pieces*

1 Lightly grease a baking sheet with
butter or oil. Mix the nuts, sugar and
water in a heavy-based saucepan. Place
the pan over a gentle heat, stirring until
all the sugar has dissolved.
2 Bring to the boil, then lower the heat to
moderate and cook until the mixture
turns a rich golden brown and registers
155°C/310°F on a sugar thermometer. If
you do not have a sugar thermometer,
test the syrup by adding a few drops to a
cup of iced water. The mixture should
solidify to a very brittle mass.

Chocolate-coated Hazelnuts
Roast about 225g/8oz/2 cups
hazelnuts in the oven or under the
grill. Allow to cool. Melt the
chocolate in a heatproof bowl over a
pan of barely simmering water.
Remove from the heat, but leave the
bowl over the water so that the
chocolate remains liquid. Have
ready about 30 paper sweet cases,
arranged on baking sheets. Add
the roasted hazelnuts to the
melted chocolate and stir to coat.
Using two spoons, carefully scoop
up a cluster of two or three
chocolate-coated nuts. Carefully
transfer the cluster to a paper sweet
case. Leave the nut clusters in a cool
place until set.

3 Quickly remove the pan from the heat
and tip the mixture on to the prepared
baking sheet, spreading it evenly. Leave
until completely cold and hard.

4 Break the nut brittle into bite-size
pieces. Melt the chocolate and dip the
pieces to half-coat them. Leave on a sheet
of non-stick baking paper to set.

COGNAC AND GINGER CREAMS

MAKES 18–20

*300g/11oz plain dark chocolate, chopped
into small pieces
45ml/3 tbsp double cream
30ml/2 tbsp cognac
4 pieces of stem ginger, finely chopped, plus
15ml/1 tbsp syrup from the jar
crystallized ginger, to decorate*

1 Polish the insides of 18–20 chocolate moulds carefully with cotton wool. Melt about two-thirds of the chocolate in a heatproof bowl over a saucepan of barely simmering water, then spoon a little into each mould. Reserve a little of the melted chocolate, for sealing the creams.

2 Using a small brush, sweep the chocolate up the sides of the moulds to coat them evenly, then invert them on to a sheet of greaseproof paper and set aside until the chocolate has set.

CHOCOLATE MARSHMALLOW DIPS
Have ready a large baking sheet lined with non-stick baking paper. Melt 175g/6oz plain or bittersweet chocolate in a heatproof bowl over barely simmering water. Stir until smooth. Remove the pan from the heat, but leave the bowl in place, so that the chocolate does not solidify too soon. You will need 15–20 large or 30–35 small marshmallows. Using cocktail sticks, spear each marshmallow and coat in the chocolate. Roll in ground hazelnuts. Place on the lined baking sheet and chill until set before removing the skewers. Place each marshmallow dip in a foil sweet case.

3 Melt the remaining chopped chocolate over simmering water, then stir in the cream, cognac, stem ginger and ginger syrup, mixing well. Spoon into the chocolate-lined moulds. If the reserved chocolate has solidified, melt, then spoon a little into each mould to seal.

4 Leave the chocolates in a cool place (not the fridge) until set. To remove them from the moulds, gently press them out on to a cool surface, such as a marble slab. Decorate with small pieces of crystallized ginger. Keep the chocolates cool if not serving them immediately.

INDEX

almonds: chocolate almond meringue pie, 34
    chocolate almond mousse cake, 15
    double-choc almond cookies, 82
apricot sauce, chocolate cones with, 60

banana, chocolate and toffee pie, 57
biscuits, 77, 82–5
black bottom pie, 46
Black Forest gâteau, 18
blackberries: rich chocolate berry tart with blackberry sauce, 43
bombes, ice cream, 70
brandy snap gâteau, chocolate, 20
brioches au chocolat, 78
brownies, white chocolate, 81

cakes: chocolate ginger crunch cake, 19
    French chocolate cake, 13
    frosted chocolate fudge cake, 19
    piping on to, 10
    white chocolate celebration cake, 24
    see also gâteaux
caramel mousse, chocolate box with, 31
Caribbean chocolate ring with rum syrup, 27
celebration cake, white chocolate, 24
cheesecakes: luxury white chocolate, 48
    marbled chocolate, 45
    raspberry, mascarpone and white chocolate, 50
cherries: Black Forest gâteau, 18
chestnut: chocolate and chestnut pie, 46
    chocolate and chestnut pots, 66
    chocolate chestnut roulade, 29
chunky chocolate bars, 75
chunky double chocolate cookies, 82
coconut: chocolate coconut roulade, 22
    white chocolate parfait, 64
coffee: chocolate tiramisu tart, 49
    mocha velvet cream pots, 66
    tiramisu in chocolate cups, 63
    white chocolate cappuccino gâteau, 23
cognac and ginger creams, 89
cream cheese: chocolate cones with apricot sauce, 60
    chocolate tiramisu tart, 49
    dark chocolate ravioli with, 37
    Italian chocolate ricotta pie, 53
    meringue gâteau with chocolate mascarpone, 14
    tiramisu in chocolate cups, 63
crêpes: chocolate crêpes with plums and port, 36
    chocolate soufflé crêpes, 38
cups, chocolate, 84
curls, piping, 11

drizzles, 10

Easter egg, truffle-filled, 94

feathering, 11
French chocolate cake, 13
frosted chocolate fudge cake, 19
frosting, chocolate, 19
fruit: chocolate box with caramel mousse and berries, 31
    chocolate sorbet with red fruits, 68
    double chocolate-dipped, 87
    steamed chocolate and fruit puddings with chocolate syrup, 33
fudge: chocolate and marshmallow, 88
    rich chocolate pistachio, 88
fudge cake, frosted chocolate, 19
fudge sundaes, chocolate, 71

galettes, chocolate hazelnut, 61
ganache, chocolate, 43
gâteaux: Black Forest gâteau, 18
    Caribbean chocolate ring with rum syrup, 27
    chocolate almond mousse cake, 15
    chocolate brandy snap gâteau, 20
    chocolate coconut roulade, 22
    chocolate redcurrant torte, 30
    meringue gâteau with chocolate mascarpone, 14
    rich chocolate leaf gâteau, 26
    Sachertorte, 16
    white chocolate cappuccino gâteau, 23
    white chocolate mousse and strawberry layer cake, 28
ginger crunch cake, chocolate, 19

hazelnuts: chocolate-coated, 90
    chocolate-dipped crescents, 77
    chocolate hazelnut galettes, 61
    hazelnut chocolate meringue torte with pears, 56

ice cream: chocolate, 72

chocolate fudge sundaes, 71
chocolate mint ice cream pie, 69
ice cream bombes, 70
rocky road ice cream, 73
white chocolate parfait, 64
Italian chocolate ricotta pie, 53

kisses, chocolate, 83

leaf gâteau, rich chocolate, 26
lemon tartlets, chocolate, 76

magic chocolate mud pudding, 35
malt whisky truffles, 93
mangoes: white chocolate and mango cream tart, 54
marbled chocolate cheesecake, 45
marbling, 11
marshmallow: chocolate and marshmallow fudge, 88
    chocolate marshmallow dips, 89
marzipan cookies, chocolate, 85
melting chocolate, 8
meringue: chocolate almond meringue pie, 34
    chocolate pavlova with passion fruit cream, 67
    hazelnut chocolate meringue torte with pears, 56
    meringue gâteau with chocolate mascarpone, 14
mint: chocolate mint ice cream pie, 69
    chocolate peppermint creams, 87
Mississippi mud pie, 52
mocha velvet cream pots, 66
mud pudding, magic chocolate, 35

nut brittle, chocolate-coated, 90

orange: chocolate and orange Scotch pancakes, 40

parfait, white chocolate, 64
pavlova with passion fruit cream, 67
pears: hazelnut chocolate meringue torte with pears, 56
    pears in chocolate fudge blankets, 41
    puffy pears, 41
pecan squares, chocolate, 80
peppermint creams, chocolate, 87
pineapple: chocolate soufflé crêpes, 38
piping chocolate, 10–11
pistachio fudge, rich chocolate, 88
plums, chocolate crêpes with, 36
profiteroles, chocolate, 59
puffy pears, 41

raspberry, mascarpone and white chocolate cheesecake, 50
ravioli, dark chocolate, 37
redcurrant torte, chocolate, 30
rocky road ice cream, 73
roulades: chocolate chestnut, 29
    chocolate coconut, 22
run-outs, 11

Sachertorte, 16
Scotch pancakes, chocolate and orange, 40
sorbet, chocolate, 68
steamed chocolate and fruit puddings with chocolate syrup, 33
storing chocolate, 9
strawberries: white chocolate mousse layer cake, 28
sundaes, chocolate fudge, 71

tarts: black bottom pie, 46
    chocolate almond meringue pie, 34
    chocolate and chestnut pie, 46
    chocolate, banana and toffee pie, 57
    chocolate lemon tartlets, 76
    chocolate mint ice cream pie, 69
    chocolate tiramisu tart, 49
    chocolate truffle tart, 44
    Italian chocolate ricotta pie, 53
    Mississippi mud pie, 52
    rich chocolate berry tart, 43
    white chocolate and mango cream tart, 54
tempering chocolate, 9
timbales, chocolate vanilla, 62
tiramisu in chocolate cups, 63
tiramisu tart, chocolate, 49
toffee and chocolate bars, 80
truffle-filled filo cups, 91
truffle tart, chocolate, 44
truffles: chocolate, 92
    malt whisky truffles, 93
    truffle-filled Easter egg, 94
tuiles, chocolate cinnamon, 84

vanilla timbales, chocolate, 62

walnuts: chocolate and toffee bars, 80
whisky truffles, 93

TRUFFLE-FILLED EASTER EGG

MAKES 1 LARGE, HOLLOW EASTER EGG

*350g/12oz plain couverture chocolate,
tempered, or plain, milk or white chocolate,
melted
Chocolate Truffles*

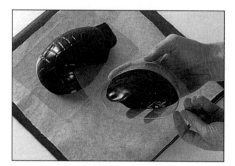

1 Line a small baking sheet with non-stick baking paper. Using a small ladle or spoon, pour in enough melted chocolate to coat both halves of an Easter egg mould. Tilt the half-moulds slowly to coat the sides completely; pour any excess chocolate back into the bowl. Set the half-moulds, open side down, on the prepared baking sheet and leave for 1–2 minutes until just set.

2 Apply a second coat of chocolate and chill for 1–3 minutes more, until set. Repeat a third time, then replace the moulds on the baking sheet and chill for at least 1 hour or until the chocolate has set completely. (Work quickly to avoid having to temper the chocolate again; untempered chocolate can be reheated if it hardens.)

4 Holding the mould open side down, squeeze firmly to release the egg half. Repeat with the other half and chill, loosely covered. (Do not touch the chocolate surface with your fingers, as they will leave prints.) Reserve any melted chocolate to reheat for "glue".

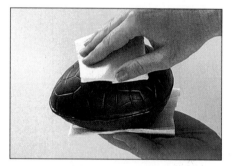

5 To assemble the egg, hold one half of the egg with a piece of folded kitchen paper or foil and fill with small truffles. If necessary, use the remaining melted chocolate as "glue". Spread a small amount on to the rim of the egg half and, holding the empty egg half with a piece of kitchen paper or foil, press it on to the filled half, making sure the rims are aligned and carefully joined.

3 To remove the set chocolate, place a half-mould, open side up, on a board. Carefully trim any drops of chocolate from the edge of the mould. Gently insert the point of a small knife between the chocolate and the mould to break the air lock. Repeat with the second mould.

6 Hold for several seconds, then prop up the egg with the folded paper or foil and chill to set. If you like, decorate the egg with ribbons or Easter decorations.

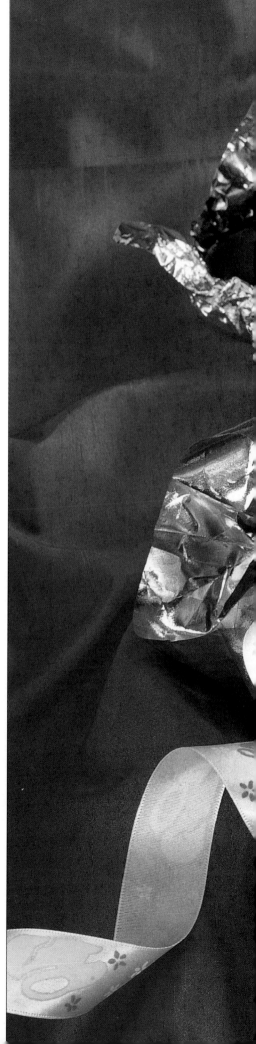

MALT WHISKY TRUFFLES

MAKES 25–30

*200g / 7oz plain dark chocolate, chopped into
small pieces
150ml / ¼ pint / ⅔ cup double cream
45ml / 3 tbsp malt whisky
115g / 4oz / ¾ cup icing sugar
cocoa powder, for coating*

1 Melt the chocolate in a heatproof bowl
over a saucepan of simmering water, stir
until smooth, then cool slightly.

2 Using a wire whisk, whip the cream
with the whisky in a bowl until thick
enough to hold its shape.

3 Stir in the melted chocolate and icing
sugar, mixing evenly, then leave until firm
enough to handle.

4 Dust your hands with cocoa powder
and shape the mixture into bite-size balls.
Coat in cocoa powder and pack into
pretty cases or boxes. Store in the fridge
for up to 3–4 days if necessary.

CHOCOLATE TRUFFLES

MAKES 20 LARGE OR 30 MEDIUM TRUFFLES

250ml/8fl oz/1 cup double cream
275g/10oz fine quality bittersweet or plain chocolate, chopped into small pieces
40g/1½oz/3 tbsp unsalted butter, cut into small pieces
45ml/3 tbsp brandy, whisky or liqueur of own choice
cocoa powder, for dusting (optional)
finely chopped pistachio nuts, to decorate (optional)
400g/14oz bittersweet chocolate, to decorate (optional)

1 Pour the cream into a saucepan. Bring to the boil over a medium heat. Remove from the heat and add the chocolate, all at once. Stir gently until melted. Stir in the butter until melted, then stir in the brandy, whisky or liqueur. Strain into a bowl and cool to room temperature. Cover the mixture with clear film and chill for 4 hours or overnight.

2 Line a large baking sheet with non-stick baking paper. Using a small ice cream scoop, melon baller or tablespoon, scrape up the mixture into 20 large balls or 30 medium balls and place on the lined baking sheet. Dip the scoop or spoon in cold water from time to time, to prevent the mixture from sticking.

3 If dusting with cocoa powder, sift a thick layer of cocoa on to a dish or pie plate. Roll the truffles in the cocoa, rounding them between the palms of your hands. (Dust your hands with cocoa to prevent the truffles from sticking.) Do not worry if the truffles are not perfectly round as an irregular shape looks more authentic. Alternatively, roll the truffles in very finely chopped pistachios. Chill on the paper-lined baking sheet until firm. Keep in the fridge for up to 10 days or freeze for up to 2 months.

4 If coating with chocolate, do not roll the truffles in cocoa, but freeze them for 1 hour. For perfect results, temper the chocolate. Alternatively, simply melt it in a heatproof bowl over a saucepan of barely simmering water. Using a fork, dip the truffles, one at a time, into the melted chocolate, tapping the fork on the edge of the bowl to shake off excess. Place on a baking sheet, lined with non-stick baking paper. If the chocolate begins to thicken, reheat it gently until smooth. Chill the truffles until set.

TRUFFLE-FILLED FILO CUPS

MAKES ABOUT 24 CUPS

3–6 sheets fresh or thawed frozen filo pastry,
depending on size
40g / 1½ oz / 3 tbsp unsalted butter, melted
sugar, for sprinkling
pared strips of lemon zest, to decorate
FOR THE CHOCOLATE TRUFFLE
MIXTURE
250ml / 8fl oz / 1 cup double cream
225g / 8oz bittersweet or plain chocolate,
chopped into small pieces
50g / 2oz / ¼ cup unsalted butter, cut into
small pieces
30ml / 2 tbsp brandy or liqueur

1 Prepare the truffle mixture. In a
saucepan over a medium heat, bring the
cream to a boil. Remove from the heat
and add the pieces of chocolate, stirring
until melted. Beat in the butter and add
the brandy or liqueur. Strain into a bowl
and chill for 1 hour until thick.

2 Preheat oven to 200°C/400°F/Gas 6.
Grease a 12-hole bun tray. Cut the filo
sheets into 6cm / 2½ in squares. Cover
with a damp dish towel. Place one square
on a work surface. Brush lightly with
melted butter, turn over and brush the
other side. Sprinkle with a pinch of sugar.
Butter another square and place it over
the first at an angle; sprinkle with sugar.
Butter a third square and place over the
first two, unevenly, so the corners form
an uneven edge. Press the layered square
into one of the holes in the bun tray.

3 Continue to fill the tray, working
quickly so that the filo does not have time
to dry out. Bake the filo cups for 4–6
minutes, until golden. Cool for 10
minutes on the bun tray then carefully
transfer to a wire rack and cool
completely.
4 Stir the chocolate mixture; it should be
just thick enough to pipe. Spoon the
mixture into a piping bag fitted with a
medium star nozzle and pipe a swirl into
each filo cup. Decorate each with tiny
strips of lemon zest.

Asian Art

Selections from the Norton Simon Museum

Edited by Pratapaditya Pal

2

Norton Simon and Asian Art
Pratapaditya Pal

6

Buddhist Art of Northern India
Janice Leoshko

20

Hindu Sculpture of Northern India
Joseph M. Dye, III

34

Southern Indian Art
Vidya Dehejia

48

Art from the Himalayas
Robert E. Fisher

60

Art from Southeast Asia
Pratapaditya Pal

76

Maps of South and Southeast Asia

Norton Simon Museum, Pasadena, in association with *Orientations*

Norton Simon and Asian Art

Pratapaditya Pal

Mr and Mrs Norton Simon on Malibu Beach

After a visit to the well-known cave temple at Elephanta Island near Bombay in 1910, the British artist, Sir William Rothenstein, wrote:

The rock-cut entrance to the cave-temple was simple and impressive; then deep within the shadow we came upon the great Trimurti,...carved with a breadth I have never seen surpassed. Then out of the gloom emerged figures of Siva, of Siva and Parvati, and of attendant *apsaras*...We were overwhelmed by the dynamic force of these great carvings, and I returned to Bombay with a new conception of plastic arts.

Norton Simon's reaction was similar when he visited India in the summer of 1971 with his new bride, the celebrated film star Jennifer Jones, and viewed the sculptures in the National Museum, New Delhi. Mr Simon was already an international figure in industry as well as the art world. By 1970 he had been collecting European art for more than three decades and had assembled one of the greatest private collections in the world. Although primarily interested in European art, he had also acquired works from other cultures, such as Egypt and China which continue to grace his home. In 1974 Mr Simon acquired the newly built edifices of what was then known as the Pasadena Museum and established his own museum on 1 March 1975.

Mr Simon first became acquainted with Indian art in the autumn of 1969 when, as a trustee of the Los Angeles County Museum of Art (he was one of the principal motivating forces behind its foundation in 1965), he voted to acquire the famous Heeramaneck Collection. He considers that deal to have been particularly astute and significant in the history of the museum. However, it was not until his trip to India in 1971 that he became really 'hooked' on Indian sculpture. Perhaps his new wife also contributed to kindling his interest, for she has always been enthusiastic about Asian cultures in general (one remembers her outstanding portrayal of a Eura-sian girl in the film *Love is a Many Splendoured Thing*) and in yoga in particular. Although she is involved with many civic and charitable organizations and causes, she finds time to be an active trustee of the Norton Simon Museum and is keenly interested in her husband's art collections.

Once Mr Simon's interest in Indian art was aroused he became a force to be reckoned with in the art market. Within six months of his visit to India, with his characteristic zeal he acquired a large group of sculptures. As a connoisseur he was naturally drawn to them primarily for their aesthetic qualities but, being a shrewd business-man, he was also motivated by the fact

(*Opposite top*) Indian Sculpture Gallery, Norton Simon Museum

(*Opposite bottom*) Southeast Asian Sculpture Gallery, Norton Simon Museum

2

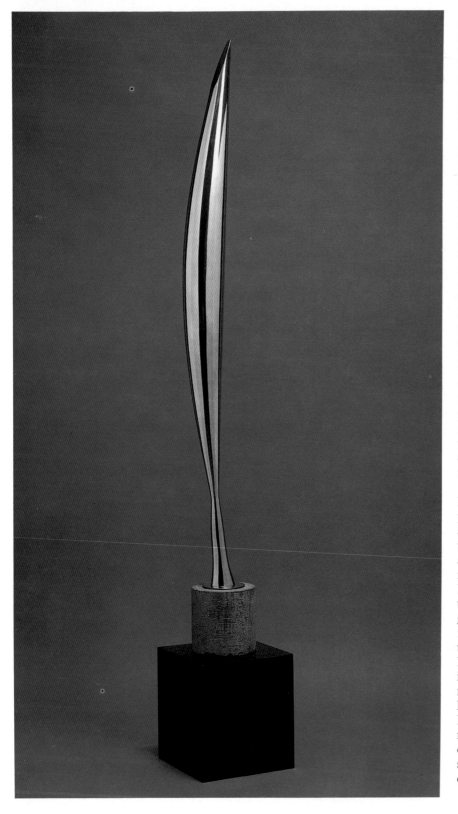

Bird in Space, dated 1931
By Constantin Brancusi (1876-1957),
Rumanian
Bronze
Height 185.5 cm
The Norton Simon Foundation

that Indian art was grossly under-priced, and still is, when compared with European art. How could one resist great sculptures selling for sums that were a fraction of the astronomical prices commanded by Old Masters or Impressionist paintings, which were Mr Simon's main field of interest.

When asked what really inspired him to become a serious collector of Indian and Southeast Asian sculptures, since all his life he had shown little interest in any other sculptural tradi-tion, Mr Simon's response was char-acteristically quick and took the form of another question. 'Why not?' he asked. 'I personally owned several Oriental pieces and were not some of the European artists I collect such as Gauguin, Picasso and others influenced by non-Western and particularly Oriental art?' This was of course true and one of the greatest twentieth-century sculptors, Auguste Rodin (who is well represented in the Norton Simon Museum) shared his enthusiasm for Chola bronzes, in particular Natarajas. Mr Simon was not aware of Rodin's admiration of the Nataraja (see Vidya Dehejia's discussion) and when pointed out by this author he was evidently pleased.

In fact, although there are numerous European as well as Asian master-pieces in the Simon collection, it was a Chola bronze Nataraja that made the headlines in the mid-seventies and brought Mr Simon international notoriety. Known as the Sivapuram Nataraja, it was the subject of litiga-tion between the collector and the government of India. The case was finally settled amicably and after being the most well-known object in the Norton Simon Museum for a decade, it was returned to India in 1986. In many ways it is a pity, for it will be lost in oblivion in India, whereas in Pasadena it was seen and admired by millions of visitors. No other single object of Indian origin had served so well as an ambassador of Indian culture.

By a strange coincidence, Norton

Simon also acquired a European sculpture that once had an interesting association with India. An abstract sculpture entitled *Bird in Space*, it was created by the Rumanian sculptor, Constantin Brancusi (1876-1957), in 1931 for the then Maharaja of Indore. The sculpture does not necessarily reflect Indian influence, but like many of his contemporary European artists, Brancusi was both familiar with and an admirer of Indian and Southeast Asian sculpture which he first encountered in the Musée Guimet in Paris. Today this museum houses the finest and most extensive holdings of Cambodian art outside of Cambodia. Although not as wide-ranging, Mr Simon's collection of Cambodian sculpture includes several outstanding examples that are equally significant and beautiful as the best pieces in Musée Guimet.

It would not be an exaggeration to

state that today the Norton Simon Museum is a major repository of the sculptural traditions of India, Nepal, Thailand and Cambodia. A large part of the collection is dramatically displayed in three galleries in the museum and also at several locations outside. Thus, unlike all other Western museum presentations, at Pasadena one can see a substantial number of sculptures in 'natural' surroundings and in natural light, which is how one sees sculptures *in situ* embellishing Indian temples. Nestled in rich green foliage and enjoying the almost perennial sunshine of Southern California, the boldly carved figures of Siva, Vishnu and the Buddha seem quite at home thousands of miles away from their original localities.

The Simon collection of South and Southeast Asian sculpture, formed in less than a decade and although less well-known than the European collec-

View of Sculpture Gallery with Nagapattinam bronze standing Buddha inside and stone seated Buddha outside (see Vidya Dehejia discussion of the Nagapattinam Buddhas)

tion, is unquestionably one of the finest and most comprehensive in the Western world. Only a fully illustrated catalogue can provide those who cannot visit the museum with an adequate idea of its scope and significance. In the meantime it is hoped that the selection discussed and illustrated here will serve as a brief but enticing introduction to an extraordinary collection.

Pratapaditya Pal is Senior Curator of Indian and Southeast Asian Art, Los Angeles County Museum of Art.

Buddhist Art of Northern India

Janice Leoshko

Spanning more than a thousand years, the Buddhist sculptures from northern India in the Norton Simon collection are remarkably varied and include some historically important and unique examples. Although it was unintentional, the collection represents significant aspects of the development of Buddhist art in northern India. It contains two well-preserved pillars from the second-century BC stupa at Bharhut, a key monument for the history of Buddhist art in particular and Indian art in general. Fewer than a dozen pieces of sculpture from this important site are known outside India, and none as impressive as these pillars. The collection is exceptionally strong in the Buddhist art of Gandhara and Mathura of the Kushan period (1st-3rd centuries), containing some monumental examples of extraordinary quality. However, there are no specimens from the Amaravati region, the other important early Indian school of Buddhist sculpture. The well-known Gupta period (*c.* 320-600) of North Indian art is also less thoroughly represented than the earlier Kushan period. There are a number of metal and stone sculptures from the Pala period (*c.* 750-1150), which witnessed the last flowering of Buddhist art in Bihar and Bengal. Another region well documented by fewer but excellent bronzes is Kashmir, which is discussed in the essay on Himalayan art by Robert E. Fisher.

Bharhut

The earliest Buddhist sculptures in the Simon collection are the two railing pillars (Figs 1 and 2) from Bharhut, Madhya Pradesh. Bharhut is one of earliest known sites where a large stupa received elaborate embellishment of its stone railing and gateways. First used by Buddhists as reliquary mounds to contain the Buddha's cremated remains, stupas were subsequently erected for other religious teachers and as a sign of the Buddha's achievement of nirvana, a reminder of the goal of all Buddhists. Most early Buddhist patronage of artistic activity was probably associated with the decoration of stupas which were a focal point for worship.

When the British archaeologist Sir Alexander Cunningham (1814-93) discovered Bharhut in 1873 he found that the stupa itself had been mostly destroyed by the local villagers who had used it as a quarry for bricks. Despite that, a number of the upright pillars and crossbeams of the railing as well as one of the four monumental gateways had survived. The Bharhut reliefs demonstrate that by the second century BC the Indian artistic vocabulary with an emphasis on the human form was already well established. However, the shallow carving of the reliefs means that the figures are not really separated from the ground, so they lack the organic quality and energy that characterize images from later periods. In addition to being among the first surviving examples of Buddhist stone sculpture, the Bharhut remains also bear important inscriptions that identify the subjects depicted and record the patronage of numerous devotees.

In the upper, larger register of one pillar (Fig. 1), a woman grasps a flowering tree with her right arm. This subject relates to a popular belief that the touch of a young woman can cause a tree to flower. Similar figures found at Bharhut and other Buddhist sites represent different types of fertility goddesses that existed before Buddhism but were incorporated into the symbolic repertoire of Buddhist art. An inscription on this pillar has been read as 'Mahakoka devata', the goddess Mahakoka. Emphasis on fertility and well-being is also conveyed by the female's left hand which seems at the same time to point to her parted legs and to the amorous couple below.

Lavishly jewelled couples were borrowed from pre-Buddhist concepts and apparently signal the abundance of material as well as the spiritual fruits associated with Buddhist practice.

Although the right side of the second pillar (Fig. 2) was cut away when reused in a modern building, enough remains to identify the continuous narrative presentation of Sakyamuni's departure from his father's palace. Born as Prince Siddhartha, Sakyamuni spent the first thirty years of his life surrounded by luxury, but with his decision to embark on a spiritual quest and seek release from the endless chain of existence, he left his father's palace. Thus, the great departure symbolizes a pivotal point in his life.

At early Buddhist monuments like Bharhut, events from the life of Sakyamuni are seemingly presented without the depiction of Sakyamuni himself. The story commences at the top with two females (perhaps deities since they stand on lotuses) in the palace and footprints at the upper right side, which signal Sakyamuni's movement to his horse led by the groom Chandaka. The horse is riderless, but the umbrella, flanked by two flywhisks positioned above the saddle, indicates a special presence. In such early reliefs elements of setting are kept to a minimum and realistic spatial concerns are disregarded. Nevertheless the walls appearing in the middle of the relief ingeniously separate the successive scenes and at the same time demonstrate that the horse depicted below has left the city. Other figures in the relief make gestures of adoration — one at the bottom plays a drum — celebrating the joyous event of Sakyamuni's decision to seek spiritual release which will then provide salvation for other living beings. Perhaps one of these figures relates to the name inscribed on the relief, 'the god Arhaguta'. This name occurs on another Bharhut relief, but it is not encountered in other images or in Buddhist texts.

(Fig. 1) Railing pillar
Madhya Pradesh, Bharhut, 2nd century BC
Sandstone
Height 147.3 cm
The Norton Simon Foundation

(Fig. 2) Railing pillar
Madhya Pradesh, Bharhut, 2nd century BC
Sandstone
Height 137.2 cm
The Norton Simon Foundation

(Fig. 3) Railing pillar
Uttar Pradesh, Mathura, 2nd century
Sandstone
Height 72.3 cm
Norton Simon Collection

Kushan Period

The Kushan period sculptures in the Simon collection admirably document the two schools of art that flourished at that time in northern India. One school existed in the area known as Gandhara, which was comprised of parts of present-day Pakistan and Afghanistan. The other school was located around Mathura, an important city on the Yamuna River in the modern Indian state of Uttar Pradesh. Although the imagery of the two schools is often similar, the styles are distinct. Mathuran art developed from earlier traditions exemplified by the Bharhut reliefs, while Gandharan art incorporated influences of Hellenistic and Roman styles, a result of political and economic contacts with the Mediterranean world.

A Kushan period railing pillar (Fig. 3) from Mathura demonstrates the continued development of traditions as the female subject relates to fertility deities encountered in the Bharhut reliefs. But the carving is substantially deeper, revealing the Mathuran artist's greater ease with sculpting stone and creating plastic forms. The physical presence of the figure is almost overwhelming and endows it with a sense of vitality. A number of pillars used in both Buddhist and Jain railings from Mathura depict such voluptuous females with small figures peering from balconies above. As decoration of religious monuments, they probably continue to signify the general auspiciousness attached to fertility spirits. The crouching dwarf on which this one stands may symbolize the subjugation of evils.

Far more impressive than the previous example and the only one of its kind in an American collection is a corner column (Figs 4 and 4a) from a Buddhist stupa. Two sides contain reliefs, and slots for the crossbars appear on the other two sides. On one side the top scene presents the death of the Buddha. The death-bed is positioned between two trees as traditionally described by Buddhist texts. Mourners appear below the bed which is depicted without the figure of the Buddha. Apparently the artist of the relief chose to continue the earlier tradition of not showing the Buddha even though Buddha figures were used in this period. On the other side the top relief shows a stupa entwined with a serpent deity. Serpent imagery, particularly as guardian figures, is a common component of Buddhist art. Below these scenes are tiers of couples who are either in devotional attitudes or hold lotus offerings, serving as symbols of the homage to be accorded in Buddhist practice. The pillar is in a remarkable state of preservation, especially its intact capital (Fig. 4a) which is shaped in the form of a miniature shrine. Since little architecture has survived at Mathura from the Kushan period, such works are valuable documents of lost architectural forms.

(Fig. 4a) Detail of Figure 4

(Fig. 4) Column with reliefs of Buddhist
scenes
Uttar Pradesh, Mathura, 2nd century
Sandstone
Height 231.1 cm
The Norton Simon Foundation

9

(Fig. 5) Fragment of a stele with relief
depiction of bodhi tree and flying attendants
Uttar Pradesh, Mathura, 2nd century
Sandstone
Height 53.2 cm, width 99 cm
The Norton Simon Foundation

Another noteworthy object from Mathura is a fragment (Fig. 5) of what must have been a very large sculpture of a seated Buddha; only the upper part of a stele remains. A halo encircling the Buddha's head would have been surmounted by the leaves which can be specifically identified by their heart-shaped form as pipal leaves. It was beneath a pipal tree that the Buddha Sakyamuni attained enlightenment. The fragmentary nature of the piece actually enhances one's appreciation of the artist's skill in rendering these leaves. This finely carved arboreal backdrop also includes small adorants who are flying, as indicated by their bent legs, to bring offerings to the Buddha.

The free-standing sculpture in Figure

6 is a forcefully modelled figure of a bodhisattva from Mathura, although its head, right arm and feet are lost. Bodhisattva images, which begin to survive in art at about the same time as Buddha images, depict beings who are capable of enlightenment but forgo it in order to help other living beings towards salvation. Often they serve as attendants to the Buddha, literally aids to his teachings. They are differentiated from Buddha figures by their princely dress and ornaments as well as by the objects they hold. The frontality of the Simon figure and the heroic proportions of the torso create a commanding presence. The sensitive modelling of the image is exceptional, providing a foretaste of the refined qualities that develop in the succeeding

(Fig. 6) Bodhisattva
Uttar Pradesh, Mathura, 2nd century
Sandstone
Height 56.2 cm
The Norton Simon Foundation

Gupta period.

A rather different and impressive presence is made by the bodhisattva image in Figure 7, which is twice the height of the Mathuran example. It comes from Gandhara and represents the other school of art that flourished during the reign of the Kushans. The bodhisattva, with only the hands and halo missing, is in remarkable condition. His lower garment and shawl with a knotted end and his numerous ornaments are types usually encountered in Gandharan bodhisattva figures. More important is the representation of Poseidon in the torque around his neck, a practice not uncommon in the Gandharan social and religious milieu. Part of the bodhisattva's hair is gathered up in

a chignon decorated by gems from which cascade short bangs and longer locks. This hairstyle is found in images that have sometimes been identified as Bodhisattva Maitreya, who usually holds a waterpot in his left hand, but since the object originally held in the left hand of this figure is lost, the identification is not secure. On the plinth appears a seated bodhisattva flanked by devotees. Also depicted in other Gandharan sculptures, this may be Sakyamuni before he became a Buddha performing his first meditation.

The sandals and the moustache, not otherwise seen in early Indian art, and the style of the sculpture reveals its debt to Greco-Roman influences even though the Western Classical

forms have become somewhat conventionalized. A comparison with the Mathuran bodhisattva establishes the differences between these contemporaneous schools. The drapery of the Gandharan bodhisattva is more naturalistically modelled and voluminous than the almost transparent dhoti worn by the Mathuran bodhisattva, and his precisely rendered musculature is quite different from the softly nuanced flesh found in Mathuran examples. Although his pose mimics the realistic stance of Western contraposto where one leg bends in relaxation, the mask-like quality of the image's facial features and its frontality keep this Gandharan bodhisattva from assuming a completely human aura.

11

(Fig. 8, *left*) Buddha
Pakistan, Gandhara, 2nd century
Schist
Height 175.2 cm
The Norton Simon Foundation

(Fig. 9, *above*) Atlas
Pakistan, Gandhara, 3rd century
Schist
Height 39.2 cm
The Norton Simon Foundation

(Fig. 7, *opposite*) Bodhisattva
Pakistan, Gandhara, 2nd century
Schist
Height 190.5 cm
The Norton Simon Foundation

Similar stylistic points can also be made about the large standing Buddha (Fig. 8) from Gandhara in the Simon collection. Again the size, condition and quality of carving make it a notable Kushan period sculpture. While stylistically different, the Gandharan Buddha displays the same iconographic traits found in Mathuran Buddha sculptures, such as elongated ears which show that he was once a prince who wore jewellery. As in Mathuran examples, he has a dot on the forehead between the eyes and the cranial protuberance, which are symbols of his supernormal wisdom. Moreover, the Gandharan Buddha, like those from Mathura, was originally adorned with a halo to indicate his spiritual aura.

While Gandharan Buddha and bodhisattva figures reveal a Western Classical influence in terms of style rather than subject, other Gandharan sculptures show Greco-Roman influence in both respects. The Simon collection contains one example which is a type of an architectural support depicting a winged Atlas (Fig. 9). A number of different forms of such Classically inspired figures survive, but this is one of the finest and largest. Usually well-developed musculature and static poses are used to emphasize the supportive function of such figures, this brawny figure of Atlas, however, is relaxed and confident of his strength.

13

(Fig. 10) Relief with Buddhist scenes
Pakistan, Gandhara, 2nd-3rd century
Schist
Height 21.6 cm, width 73.6 cm
The Norton Simon Foundation

Kushan period narrative reliefs from Mathura continue the simplified treatment seen at Bharhut and are relatively few in number, but Gandharan sculptors, inspired by Classical models, delighted in complex compositions and naturalistic representations (Fig. 10). Such reliefs served as decorations on façades of the lower portions of the many stupas and other architectural structures found in monasteries of the region. The decorative motifs used in these reliefs, like the Atlas figure, are often derived from Classical traditions, as is the mode of representation. Even though the themes are Indian, the naturalistic poses and varied gestures employed in these reliefs especially aid their vivid narrative quality.

Typically, scenes relating to different stories are separated by pilasters. In the relief of Figure 10 scenes from two stories are shown. On the left side the Buddha is depicted taming a serpent in the city of Rajgir. The story concerns a selfish rich man who buried his wealth in his backyard. After he died, he was reborn as a serpent who lived in the yard and terrorized the neighbourhood in order to protect the buried treasure. In response to pleas from King Bimbisara, who is perhaps the richly dressed figure on the right, the Buddha quells the serpent. Here

the Buddha is holding his begging bowl, from which hangs the serpent, over a mound that symbolizes the garden. Vajrapani, a frequent attendant of the Buddha, appears behind him. The right side of the relief depicts another serpent tale. In this case the Buddha is presenting a serpent that he has calmed to some ascetics in the town of Uruvilva. One ascetic recoils in horror at the sight of this once fearsome snake now coiled up in the Buddha's begging bowl. Again Vajrapani stands behind the Buddha. Other ascetics, identifiable by their scanty dress, beards and hair in topknots, witness this amazing event. It is interesting that although these two stories appear fairly frequently in Gandharan art, they are rarely encountered elsewhere in the Buddhist world.

Gupta Period

During the rule of the Guptas in northern India from the fourth to the sixth centuries, although places like Mathura continued to be important, new centres of art rose to prominence. Of particular importance for Buddhist art was Sarnath located in Uttar Pradesh. Sculptures produced there represent a culmination in the development of the Buddha image, and these creations of unknown Sarnath artists exerted an enormous influence on art produced elsewhere in India and Asia, which is reflected in some of the images discussed in the essay on Simon's Southeast Asian collection

by Pratapaditya Pal.

Although the Simon collection does not contain many Gupta period Buddhist images, a rather large bronze Buddha (Fig. 11) quintessentially illustrates the qualities of the refined style associated with Sarnath. Gupta period Buddhas are famous for their harmony of form and content. Unlike the forceful physical presence encountered in Kushan period sculptures such as the Gandharan Buddha of Figure 8, the exalted state of enlightenment is visually manifested in later Buddha images by simple yet elegant modelling of the human form to convey tranquillity and introspection.

The Simon Buddha is an especially significant work since relatively few bronzes of the period have survived. The Buddha would have originally stood on a base, and a halo would have encircled his head. The tenon for fastening the halo still remains on the back of the figure. The slender proportions of the slightly swaying figure are enhanced by the gentle sweep of the robe hanging gracefully down each side. The delicate modelling of the face and the downcast eyes are characteristics of the Gupta style, but the slight elongation of the torso relates this bronze to later stylistic developments, making a date of the late sixth century most likely. Unfortunately, an exact provenance cannot be determined for the sculpture. It could have been made somewhere in Uttar Pradesh or further east in the state of Bihar where it has been suggested that other similar bronzes

14

were produced.

Another example of the refined style of Gupta period sculptures is the lower portion of a stone sculpture (Fig. 12) that probably depicted a Buddha although only the lotus pedestal on which he stood and his feet remain. At the base are arranged six kneeling male and female devotees and two standing male adorants holding garlands. Issuing from either side of the lotus are two more lotus stems that probably supported bodhisattvas. Made of flecked red sandstone characteristic of Mathuran sculptures, this work is quite similar to two complete sculptures dating from the late fifth century.

(Fig. 11, *right*) Buddha
Uttar Pradesh or Bihar, 6th century
Bronze
Height 41.9 cm
The Norton Simon Foundation

(Fig. 12) Fragment of a Buddha
Uttar Pradesh, Mathura, 5th century
Sandstone
Height 61 cm, width 71 cm
The Norton Simon Foundation

(Fig. 13) Avalokiteshvara
Bihar, Nalanda, 9th century
Bronze
Height 16.5 cm
The Norton Simon Foundation

(Fig. 14) Crowned Buddha
Bihar, Kurkihar (?), 11th century
Bronze
Height 17.8 cm
The Norton Simon Foundation

Pala Period

The last major period of Buddhist practice was in eastern India, a region comprising the present-day Indian states of Bihar and West Bengal and the nation of Bangladesh. During the Pala period, eastern India witnessed intense religious activity which resulted in the creation of an enormous amount of art, both Hindu and Buddhist.

The earliest Pala period Buddhist sculpture in the Simon collection is a small bronze depicting the bodhisattva Avalokiteshvara (Fig. 13). Its provenance can be securely identified as Nalanda, a well-known site in Bihar which was an important monastic institution during the Pala period and a principal centre of art; this attribution is based on a number of very similar bronzes from the ninth century that have been excavated from the site. The relative simplicity of this sculpture

reflects an early stage in the formation of the Pala style. Pala images are indebted to art from the Gupta period, but the softness in modelling and the restraint in decorative detailing, characteristics of Gupta images, give way in the development of Pala art to more abstracted and attenuated forms and more embellished surfaces.

As the personification of compassion, Avalokiteshvara is immensely popular throughout the Buddhist world. Among images of bodhisattvas from eastern India, Avalokiteshvara is the most frequently portrayed. With one hand holding a lotus, a symbol of compassion, and the other making a gesture of giving, this image represents the bodhisattva's simplest and most common form. Other than the facial features which are worn from rubbing by worshippers, the work is in good condition. Especially noteworthy is the small umbrella still attached to the top

of the halo, a feature that has rarely survived in other Nalanda bronzes.

Another important site in Bihar was Bodhgaya, the place where the Buddha achieved enlightenment. It is during the Pala period that the site seems to have been most active in terms of artistic production, with the most common type of Buddha image produced in the period directly relating to this site. An eleventh-century sculpture (Fig. 15) in the Simon collection is an example of this form and may have come from Bodhgaya as it is similar to others still located there. The sculpture depicts the Buddha making the gesture of touching the earth (*bhumisparsa mudra*) which refers to the event of the Buddha overcoming Mara, the god of death and desire, by calling upon the earth to witness his right to enlightenment. This took place while Sakyamuni was seated beneath the pipal tree at Bodhgaya immediately

16

(Fig. 15) Buddha with bodhisattvas
Bihar, Bodhgaya (?), 11th century
Basalt
Height 68 cm
The Norton Simon Foundation

before his enlightenment.

Although the event was illustrated in reliefs from the Kushan period, it became a common image type only in the Pala period. Certain changes in the Buddhist religion and perhaps increased activity at Bodhgaya may account for the greater popularity of this form at that time. Unlike Kushan reliefs from Gandhara, which portray the scene as a struggle between the forces of Mara and the Buddha, little sense of narrative is present in most Pala period depictions. Instead the abstract concept of enlightenment is emphasized in such images; in this stele only the Buddha's gesture and branches of the pipal tree remain as specific references to the event.

No bronze images have yet been found at Bodhgaya, but the nearby site of Kurkihar has yielded a number of spectacular examples. Kurkihar was the site of a large monastic community as well as a significant art centre. A bronze Buddha (Fig. 14) in the Simon collection relates to others that were accidentally found at Kurkihar in a hoard in the early part of this century. The form of the Buddha wearing a crown and necklace over his monastic robes became popular late in the Pala period, the Kurkihar crowned Buddhas all date from the late eleventh century. The form was probably meant to emphasize the cosmic rather than historical nature of the Buddha Sakyamuni, reflecting the increasing complexity which developed in the meaning of images at this time.

(Fig. 16) Goddess Tara
Bihar, Kurkihar (?), late 9th century
Chlorite
Height 91.5 cm
The Norton Simon Foundation

Even though Kurkihar has yet to be scientifically excavated a number of stone sculptures have been recovered from the site. While many of the bronzes date from the end of the Pala period, the majority of the known stone sculptures from Kurkihar belong to the ninth or tenth centuries. In the collection a ninth-century stone sculpture depicting the Buddhist goddess Tara (Fig. 16) may well be from Kurkihar. Tara was especially venerated as a goddess of great compassion who aids devotees in overcoming difficulties and was widely worshipped in eastern India. Although

Tara has a number of different forms, the most common is the one presented here holding a blue lotus and extending the right hand in the gesture of charity. She is accompanied by a male guardian attendant and a devotee who kneels clasping his hands in homage. The Buddhist creed is inscribed in the halo, a popular feature in Pala period images. This finely sculpted work is one of the most enchanting sculptures of Tara to survive.

A number of excellent Pala period sculptures in the Simon collection document the strong artistic activity that occurred at sites in the Bengal region, east of Bihar, such as an eleventh-century stone sculpture (Fig. 17) from Bengal. This impressive image depicts the bodhisattva of wisdom, Manjusri, in his form as Manjuvajra. A comparison with the ninth-century Tara clearly illustrates the stylistic developments that occurred in the late Pala period. The complicated form of Manjuvajra, who sits with multiple arms in a flaming aura etched onto the back of the stele, also reflects the growing complexity of imagery at this time, a result of Tantric Buddist practices.

Manjuvajra is encircled by four goddesses who thus form a mandala with him in the centre; a duplicate of his form appears at the top of the stele. Manjuvajra would have been the focus of meditations by devotees trying to achieve the experience of true reality — the realization that the enlightened state was the permanent condition of all beings which only ignorance and confusion kept one from knowing. In his front pair of hands the bodhisattva holds the bell and the thunderbolt (*vajra*), ritual implements that signify the nonduality of enlightenment. His other hands hold a sword with which to cut through delusion, a gem to symbolize the riches of knowledge and a blue lotus, his traditional symbol.

From the simple images of fertility deities to complex forms such as the Manjuvajra, which reflect spectacular religious visions that took centuries to develop, the Buddhist sculptures collected by Norton Simon admirably document the breadth of northern Indian Buddhist art. Not only does the collection include works from the major Buddhist centres of northern India, but many of these individual sculptures are by themselves outstand-

ing examples of Buddhist art that reflect both the ingenuity and piety of unknown master sculptors of the past.

Janice Leoshko is Assistant Curator of Indian and Southeast Asian Art, Los Angeles County Museum of Art.

Suggested further reading

Frederick Asher, *The Art of Eastern India, 300-800*, Minneapolis, 1980.
Ananda Coomaraswamy, *La Sculpture de Bharhut*, Paris, 1951.
Stanislaw J. Czuma with Rekha Morris, *Kushan Sculpture: Images from Early India*, Cleveland, 1985.

(Fig. 17) Manjuvajra
Bengal, late 11th century
Chlorite
Height 70.9 cm
The Norton Simon Foundation

Susan L. Huntington, *The 'Pāla-Sena' Schools of Sculpture*, Leiden, 1984.
Debala Mitra, *Buddhist Monuments*, Calcutta, 1971.
Pratapaditya Pal et al, *Light of Asia: Buddha Sakyamuni in Asian Art*, Los Angeles, 1984.
Joanna Gottfried Williams, *The Art of Gupta India*, Princeton, New Jersey, 1982.
Wladimer Zwalf, ed., *Buddhism: Art and Faith*, London, 1985.

Hindu Sculpture of Northern India

Joseph M. Dye, III

The Norton Simon collection of Indian art is justly famed for its spectacular metal sculptures from Kashmir and Tamil Nadu. Less well known, however, are the numerous northern Indian Hindu stone and bronze sculptures in the collection, although many of these works are of high quality and great art historical interest. They are more than a group of impressive 'trophies' and scholarly curiosities; the collection's true strength lies in its relatively comprehensive presentation of the distinctive themes and symbolic configurations that have defined Hindu art for many centuries. Norton Simon's holdings include images of voluptuous celestial maidens, passionate loving couples and nurturing mother goddesses. There are representations of the gods in their fully anthropomorphic forms as well as those that combine the shapes of man and animal, man and serpent, and man and abstract symbol. Indeed, when taken as a whole, Norton Simon's sculptures offer a vivid introduction to the fabulous imagery and rich emotional 'flavour' that make Hindu myth and art what they are.

Most Hindu sculptures are cult images of the religion's major gods, although representations of minor divinities and mythological narratives were also produced. Today, art historians approach Brahmanical sculptures such as those in the Simon collection primarily as interesting aesthetic expressions; but it is important to realize that they were originally intended to serve as objects of worship in Hindu temples and shrines. They were believed to be concrete forms or vessels in which the Hindu gods temporarily resided when they were respectfully requested to appear in the everyday world. By seeing and touching various parts of an image, the devotee was able to communicate with a deity and to become one with him.

Because of their religious function, every feature of these sacred images, particularly those belonging to the later periods, was carefully regulated. Specific attributes, hand gestures (*mudras*) and postures (*asanas*) were assigned to each deity; they revealed his various powers and energies and helped a devotee to identify him. Since the Hindu gods belonged to a level of existence that differed from everyday reality, their bodies were fashioned according to a divine rather than earthly set of proportions. Often they were represented with special physical characteristics, such as multiple arms and heads, to remind devotees that they were infinitely more powerful than ordinary mortals.

Kushan Period

The earliest works in the Simon collection that might be construed as Hindu were produced in the vicinity of Mathura during the Kushan period (1st-3rd centuries). Artists from this region and period produced some of the first known stone representations of the Hindu gods; and, as one would expect at such an early date, the iconography of these images was not always firmly established. Among the Simon collection's most powerful works from Kushan Mathura are two monumental images carved in mottled red sandstone, one depicting a Nagaraja (serpent-king). Nagas are serpent deities who are associated with the waters and who are said to guard treasures that lie deep within the earth. Honoured by Buddhists, Hindus and Jains, they may have also been the focus of an independent cult in Kushan Mathura.

The Simon Nagaraja (Fig. 1) is a damaged, but still impressive, larger-than-life-sized cult image. Originally, the figure must have stood with his feet firmly planted on the ground. His lowered left hand may have held a flask or pot containing an elixir; his right hand was possibly placed in *abhaya mudra* (gesture of reassurance). Although damaged and effaced, the sculpture possesses a remarkable sense of vigorous, robust monumentality. Its open, smiling face, square shoulders, breath-inflated chest and massively proportioned body are typical of the best Kushan sculpture from first and second-century Mathura.

(Fig. 1, *opposite*) Nagaraja
Uttar Pradesh, Mathura, *c.* 100
Sandstone
Height 213.3 cm
The Norton Simon Foundation

20

(Fig. 2, *opposite*) Balarama
Uttar Pradesh, Mathura, early 2nd century
Sandstone
Height 160 cm
The Norton Simon Foundation

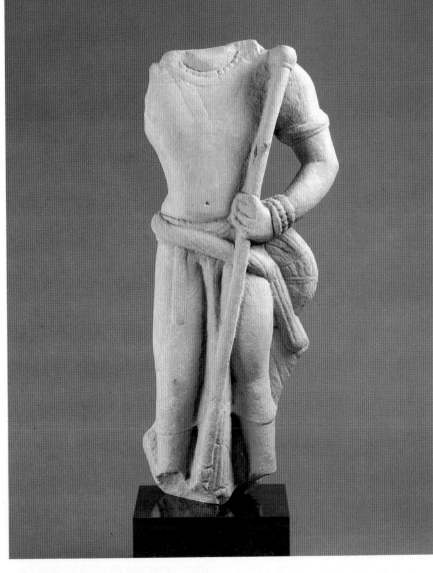

Much better preserved, though less awesome, is another sculpture (Fig. 2) that closely resembles a well-known Nagaraja image from Chargaon dated by inscription to the fortieth year of the Kanishka era, corresponding perhaps to the first quarter of the second century. This figure is frequently identified as a Nagaraja, but it is more likely that it actually represents Balarama, the elder brother of Krishna, whose cult was particularly popular in Kushan Mathura. A divinity fond of drink, Balarama is usually depicted with a wine cup, rather than the pot or flask more commonly associated with nagas.

Sensuous and heroic, the Simon figure stands against a coiling serpent, whose multiple heads form a protective canopy over the image. His right hand is raised in a gesture characteristic of a universal monarch (*chakravartin*) in ancient India; his left hand holds a stemmed cup. All the elements of this sculpture are superbly integrated: the transitions between the legs, torso and arms effortlessly melt into one another; the undulating serpent coils echo and balance the figure's swelling contraposto; and the radiating hood seems to focus and expand the exuberant self-confidence of the smiling face and raised right arm.

This figural type, one in which the deity is represented as a graceful 'giant', was repeatedly employed by Mathuran sculptors to represent both Hindu and Buddhist gods. It may be seen in another interesting Kushan sculpture (Fig. 3), a fragmentary image of a male divinity holding a large, now-damaged spear in his left hand. The spear is an important attribute of the Hindu god Kumara, but it is also held by Kubera as well as by other West Asian warrior deities. Since the Simon fragment lacks any other identifying characteristics, it is difficult to determine which of these deities it depicts. Probably it represents Kumara (also known as Kartikeya or Skanda), a complex divinity who was, among other things, the eternal youth and the god of war. Many images of Kumara were produced in the Kushan dominions: those from Mathura usually show him as a princely, dhoti-clad youth standing with a spear in his hand and, sometimes, in association with a rooster or cock; those from Gandhara depict him with the same attributes but dressed in armour.

(Fig. 3) Torso of Kumara
Uttar Pradesh, Mathura, *c.* 200
Sandstone
Height 59.7 cm
The Norton Simon Foundation

23

Gupta Period

The Gupta period (*c.* 320-600), which followed the Kushan period, is generally regarded as one of the most sophisticated, creative and influential ages in the entire history of Indian art. As Ananda K. Coomaraswamy has said:

With a new definition, it [Gupta art] establishes the classical phase of Indian art, at once serene and energetic, spiritual and voluptuous. The formulae of Indian taste are now more definitely crystallised and universally accepted; iconographic types, and compositions, still variable in the Kushan period, are now standardized in forms whose influence extended far beyond the Ganges valley, and of which the influence was felt, not only throughout India and Ceylon, but far beyond the confines of India proper, surviving to the present day.

The nature of the transition from the Kushan to the Gupta style can be grasped at least partially by comparing a fourth-century Nagini image (snake goddess; Fig. 4) from central India with the previously discussed Nagaraja sculpture from Mathura. The Gupta Nagini retains the general configuration, frontality and monumentality of the earlier image, but its mood is almost entirely different. Gone are the extroversion and sense of earthly well-being that characterized the Kushan cult image. In their place are a new, elegant aloofness and a smoother, more rationalized figural style. Instead of gazing self-confidently out into the world, the Gupta Nagini, with lowered eyes, looks serenely introspective.

(Fig. 4) Nagini
Uttar Pradesh, Mathura, 4th century
Sandstone
Height 167.6 cm
The Norton Simon Foundation

24

Much the same sense of poised inner tranquillity can be seen in a beautiful Gupta image of a mother goddess (Fig. 5), also from central India. Sitting gracefully with her legs spread wide and her breasts full, she embraces an infant, for it is the life-giving, nurturing role of a mother, rather than her envious, angry or fault-finding qualities, that are emphasized in this representation. Mother goddesses were frequently depicted in Hindu, Jain and Buddhist art of the Gupta era. This image, however, is rather unusual for the period because the goddess is shown with four, rather than two, hands. Moreover, the lower right hand holds the hilt of a sword — a somewhat curious feature for a deity otherwise depicted as a benign mother.

Another interesting Gupta sculpture in the Simon collection, a sixth century image of the god Kubera (Fig. 6), is as dignified as the previously mentioned mother goddess, but not as self-absorbed. One of the four Great Kings and the Eight Guardians of the Universe, Kubera is the god of wealth and the leader of the yakshas (nature spirits) believed to possess power over wealth and fertility. The Simon Kubera conforms to standard Gupta iconographic conventions in that it shows this lord of earthly riches as a pot-bellied, gnome-like god bearing a wine cup in his left hand and a treasure sack in his right. His head is wrapped with a rakishly asymmetrical turban. Like many other Gupta images of Kubera, the figure is seated almost on his haunches, though a low stool is delineated at the back of the relief. This earthy, expansive pose emphasizes the god's enormous pot belly and endows his figure with a certain settled dignity.

(Fig. 5, *top*) Mother goddess
Uttar or Madhya Pradesh, 6th century
Sandstone
Height 51 cm
The Norton Simon Foundation

(Fig. 6) Kubera
Uttar Pradesh, 6th century
Sandstone
Height 51 cm
The Norton Simon Foundation

Medieval Period

The memory of the Gupta achievement lingered long in North India. Its impact is clearly evident, for example, in the asymmetrical headdress and rotund, but weightless, body of a charming seventh-century figure of Ganesa (Fig. 7), the elephant-headed god of auspiciousness. During the six centuries that followed the collapse of the dynasty *circa* 600, Hindu sculpture blossomed into full flower all over the sub-continent. Many regional schools of art flourished in different parts of northern and eastern India. Most post-Gupta and Medieval Hindu stone sculpture was carved to embellish the walls and chambers of magnificent stone and brick temples erected to the major gods of Hinduism; smaller, but equally powerful, bronze sculptures were also made for worship in shrines and domestic altars. The hundreds of anonymous artists who fashioned these sacred images worked according to aesthetic norms and iconographic conventions that were, by this time, far more firmly established than they had been in the Kushan period.

The most popular themes depicted by North and East Indian artists of the Medieval period were those associated with the major deities of later Hinduism — Siva, Vishnu and Devi. Although they shared many of the same traits, each divinity had an individual nature and a distinctive iconography. The most complex and ambiguous of the three was the Great God, Siva. He was believed by his devotees to be the root and support of the universe, and the creative-destructive flow of life that rushed through it. Because he embodied all of life's processes and paradoxes, Siva was depicted in a wide variety of codified iconographic forms, each one of which captured an aspect of his complex personality. Some of these

images show him in his different anthropomorphic forms, for example, as an ascetic, a dancer or a demon-slayer; others depict him in his animal form such as the bull, still others as symbols.

Perhaps the most distinctive form used to represent Siva, however, was the linga, the abstract sign or symbol of the Great God. A large, pillar-like shaft with a curved top, the linga served as the main object of worship in temples dedicated to Siva. Sometimes it was carved with one or more of the Great God's faces. Two such *mukha* ('face') lingas rendered in different styles, but of the same high quality, are included in the Simon collection. The first, a fine one-face (*ekamukha*) linga (Fig. 8) from ninth-century Bihar, was carved in a regional style that emphasized tightly ordered

(Fig. 7) Ganesa
Uttar Pradesh, 7th century
Sandstone
Height 81.2 cm
The Norton Simon Foundation

forms and crisply rendered detail. It is hardly surprising then, that each strand of the god's hair and every bead of his necklace are carefully noted; their precision is echoed in the hard line that defines the eyes, fleshy lips and geometric eyebrows. These elements are firmly locked into place by the strong vertical axis established by the deity's parted hair, third eye and now-damaged nose. The intense power of the Great God's large-featured face is summed up in the steady, forceful gaze of his eyes.

26

(Fig. 8) One-face linga
Bihar, 9th century
Chlorite
Height 48.3 cm
The Norton Simon Foundation.

(Fig. 9) Five-face linga
Uttar Pradesh, 9th century
Sandstone
Height 44 cm
The Norton Simon Foundation

Although of roughly the same date, the second *mukhalinga* (Fig. 9) in the Simon collection was produced by central Indian artists who worked in a far less assertive style than those from ninth-century Bihar. This linga belongs to the 'five-face' (*panchamukha*) linga class. It consists of a central shaft around which are carved four different heads of Siva. Each head has its own name and faces in one of the four cardinal directions; the fifth head is not represented for it is believed to be symbolically present at the top of the linga. Smooth and tightly modelled, the faces of this example are ripe with sensuous appeal. All of them, except that of Siva as the angry Aghora-Bhairava, are shown with highly arched, tendril-like brows, lowered eyelids, and full lower lips relaxed in the state of blissful meditation.

27

The abstract aspects of the Simon lingas are, in many respects, typical of Saivite myths and iconography which tended to emphasize the Great God as an embodiment of remote, cosmic processes and mystical, universal paradoxes. Far more concrete and immediate was the imagery used by North and East Indian Medieval sculptors to depict Siva's antithesis — Vishnu, the Pervader. A kind and dependable god, he was believed to work continually for the world's welfare. Many of this respectable deity's benign qualities are captured in a richly detailed bronze shrine now in the Simon collection (Fig. 10). Cast in

northern central India, this superb Pratihara period (8th-11th centuries) sculpture is unusually large and very rare. Vishnu and Lakshmi, his consort, stand in warm embrace at the centre of the composition. He touches her breast with tender affection; both of them face the devotee, smiling.

The dense, intricately wrought arch that surrounds the blissful couple teems with mythical animals, flying celestials and iconic representations of the gods. Included among these heavenly 'courtiers' are diminutive depictions of the avatars (descents or incarnations) of Vishnu. It is said in Hindu texts that whenever the universe was in danger of total destruction at the hands of evil demons, Vishnu assumed a bodily form and descended to the world to save it. Traditionally, there were ten avatars of Vishnu: Fish; Tortoise; Man-Lion (Narasimha); Vamana the Dwarf (also known as Trivikrama); Rama with a Battle Axe; Rama; Krishna; Buddha; and Kalki, the incarnation yet to come.

Among the Simon collection's many North and East Indian Medieval representations of Vishnu's avatars, three examples stand out as being particularly successful. Each one of these reliefs emphasizes a different aspect of Vishnu's cosmic power and demonstrates Medieval Hindu sculpture's extraordinary intellectual depth and emotional range. A late tenth or early eleventh-century Bengali image of Vishnu in his Narasimha avatar (Fig. 11) depicts a moment when the normally benign god suddenly turned into a deadly killer. Vishnu assumed this form to destroy the demon-king Hiranyakasipu, who was immune from attacks by men, animals and gods, and who could be killed neither by day or night, nor inside or outside his palace. The ignorant demon-king's eventual destruction at the hands of Vishnu as Narasimha is depicted with compelling intensity in the Simon stele. At the centre of the composition, the Narasimha brutally rips open Hiranyakasipu's abdomen. Intestines, rendered with morbid accuracy, spill out of his nude, vulnerable body. The demon raises a sword in his right hand, but his feet, dangling and lifeless, already proclaim his ultimate fate. Nothing can resist Vishnu's destructive energy: radiating from his composite form, it fills his bristling mane, skull-like head and staring eyes with terrifying intensity.

(Fig. 11) Narasimha avatar of Vishnu
Bengal, *c.* 1000
Chlorite
Height 118.3 cm
The Norton Simon Foundation

29

(Fig. 12, *opposite*) Vamana avatar of Vishnu
Bengal, 11th century
Chlorite
Height 144.8 cm
The Norton Simon Collection

(Fig. 13) Rama avatar of Vishnu
Rajasthan, *c.* 1000
Sandstone
Height 219 cm
The Norton Simon Foundation

The Narasimha image dramatically depicts Vishnu's avenging destructiveness, but the second Simon avatar relief (Fig. 12) emphasizes his awesome grandeur. This eleventh-century sculpture, also from Bengal, depicts Vishnu at the moment when he, as Vamana the Dwarf (Trivikrama), grew to colossal size and, in three great strides, recovered the universe from the overweening King Bali. Unlike the dynamic Narasimha relief, in which most standard peripheral elements are eliminated to emphasize the god's ferocious destruction, this stele is treated as though it were an elaborate Hindu cult icon: detached and majestic, Vishnu stands at the centre of the composition, flanked by symmetrically arranged attendants and flying figures. Apart from the diminutive representation of an earlier moment in the myth appearing near the god's feet, and the arrangement of standard Vaishnava attributes, only the raised left leg of the god boldly announces to the devotee that this relief represents the Three Strides.

The two Pala reliefs from Bengal depict avatars of Vishnu which though frequently represented, never did attain the popularity that the god's seventh incarnation, Rama, did in later Hinduism. Vishnu assumed this form in order to quell the evil demon-king Ravana, a myth that forms the subject of the great Hindu epic, the *Ramayana*. An image of Rama (Fig. 13) in the Simon collection carved in tenth or eleventh-century Rajasthan is extraordinary, not only for its quality but also for its larger-than-life size. Standing in a contraposto pose, the noble god leans against his bow, which rises like an undulating ribbon, up the left side of his body. The feather tips of his arrows, doubtlessly carried in a quiver, although not visible, radiate from his shoulders. Unlike the Pala reliefs which, each in its own way, depicts a specific moment in the avatar's myth, this sculpture shows Rama in a timeless, iconic form.

(Fig. 14, *above*) Surya with attendants
Bengal, 8th century
Bronze
Height 19 cm
The Norton Simon Foundation

(Fig. 15) Celestial nymph
Rajasthan (?), 10th century
Sandstone
Height 81.2 cm
The Norton Simon Foundation

The development of Vishnu's personality and iconography, like that of most Hindu deities, evolved over a long period of time. At first, Vishnu was simply one of several early solar deities. Later, the Sun god, Surya, came to be regarded by followers of Vishnu as merely an aspect of their god. A Pala dynasty bronze image of Surya (Fig. 14) is noteworthy for its early date and great rarity. The god's now-broken hands once held the stalks of lotuses, the blossoms of which unfold near his shoulders. He is flanked by Danda, his measurer, and by Pingala, the recorder; the small figure of a donor, appearing on the lower left corner of the base, kneels before the deities in respectful adoration. The boots worn by the three deities are a survival from the iconography of the Kushan period when Surya is always shown in such foot gear.

Iconic images of the gods, with their elaborately standardized forms and codified gestures, were the most important, but certainly not the only subjects depicted by North and East Indian Medieval artists. Hindu sculpture from this region and period also abounds with lively representations of minor celestials, plants, animals and men, for they too had a place within the expansive boundaries of Hindu religion and art. Particularly beautiful are the numerous figures of celestial women known by many names — Surasundari, Alasakanya, Akarsini and others — who formed the entourages of the great gods. These voluptuous temptresses were carved on the outside walls of Hindu temples to attract devotees to the deity whose image dwelt deep inside the shrine.

Two sculptures in the Simon collection reveal the radically varied approaches taken by sculptors from different regions of Medieval North and East India to convey the voluptuous appeal of these celestial nymphs. The sensuality of the first (Fig. 15), a self-absorbed temptress from tenth-century northern central India, is beautifully expressed in the gently undulating rhythms that with superb fluency course through her body. By comparison, the second sculpture (Fig. 16), an eleventh-century flying or dancing celestial from Rajasthan, is far more dramatic but ultimately less sensual. Seized by an exaggerated intensity, her figure is pulled in dramatically contrasting directions. So overstated is her pose that the fully revealed and emphasized erotic areas are almost totally devoid of appeal.

Much larger and perhaps more beautiful than either of these images is a figure (Fig. 17) of Amazonian proportions from thirteenth-century Orissa in East India. The figure is so deeply carved that she almost seems to step forth from the back of the relief; her volumetric proportions and sinuous outline, all typical of this region and date, serve to heighten this illusion of independence. Although meticulously

picked out, the jewellery and garments are so lightly carved that they accent, rather than obscure, the smooth modelling and amplitude of the torso and limbs. Neither self-absorbed and calculated, nor arid and intense, this languid maiden awaits the devotee with the promise of total surrender.

Joseph M. Dye, III, is Curator of Asiatic Art, Virginia Museum of Fine Arts, Richmond, Virginia.

Suggested further reading

Ananda K. Coomaraswamy, *History of Indian and Indonesian Art*, reprint, New York, 1985.

Roy C. Craven, *A Concise History of Indian Art*, New York, 1976.

Stella Kramrisch, *Indian Sculpture*, reprint, Delhi, Varanasi and Patna, 1981.

Pratapaditya Pal, *Indian Sculpture*, vol. 1, Berkeley, Los Angeles and London, 1986.

Benjamin Rowland, *The Art and Architecture of India: Buddhist, Hindu, Jain*, 7th ed., Harmondsworth, 1977.

(Fig. 16, *left*) Celestial dancer
Uttar Pradesh (?), 11th century
Sandstone
Height 91.4 cm
The Norton Simon Collection

(Fig. 17) Celestial nymph
Orissa, 13th century
Stone
Height 123.2 cm
The Norton Simon Foundation

Southern Indian Art

Vidya Dehejia

Norton Simon has been well-known for many years as an eminent collector of European art, but the most publicized single object in his collection was a South Indian image of dancing Siva (Nataraja). This bronze sculpture, from a temple at Sivapuram, became the subject of a celebrated court case between the government of India and Norton Simon, who finally volunteered to return the bronze to India after he had displayed it in his museum for ten years. Although the Nataraja was the best-known Indian sculpture in the Norton Simon collection, those that remain still constitute one of the finest collections of South Indian sculptures in the world, both for their variety of styles and aesthetic appeal. Made from stone and metal, the religious sculptures are largely from Karnataka and Tamil Nadu, and range in date from the ninth to the seventeenth century. The bronze collection is certainly the most significant outside India, covering both the Chola (c. 880-1279) and Vijayanagar (14th-16th centuries) periods, and containing a remarkable variety of images including various forms of Siva and his consort Parvati, Vishnu and his two wives, Krishna, Lakshmana, Ganesa, the Buddha and the Saiva saints.

Four of the sculptures discussed here are from Karnataka, having been created in the later Chalukyan (9th-11th centuries) and succeeding Hoysala (1111-1326) periods. Two impressive stone sculptures from Tamil Nadu date from the end of Pallava rule (6th-9th centuries), but the majority of the images were created during the great Chola period of South Indian history. The art of the succeeding Vijayanagar dynasty is represented in this article by two bronzes of the fifteenth century.

Stone sculptures of deities were created to serve as icons of worship placed within shrines and, more often, to adorn the exterior walls of temples. In the Karnataka region, it is customary to find as many as a hundred stone images of the various gods decorating the walls of a single temple. Further south in Chola territory, where architects showed a greater appreciation of the value of plain surfaces, temples had fewer figures, but these were generally much larger. Images were carved from single blocks of stone and then inserted into the niches prepared for them on the temple walls. The monumental scale of the sculptures in the Simon collection serves as a forcible reminder that South India is a land where major stone temples existed in profusion.

South Indian bronzes were reproduced by the *cire perdue* ('lost wax') method, in which the figure is first modelled in hard beeswax down to the finest detail, and then encased in clay and fired. Melted wax ran out of a spout left in the clay, resulting in a hollow mould which was subsequently filled with molten metal. When cool, the mould was broken open to reveal the finished image. Thus each piece was unique and could never be exactly replicated. In the tenth and eleventh centuries, when the art of bronze-casting in the Chola workshops was at a peak, few finishing touches were required, since details had been perfected on the wax form itself. From the twelfth century onwards, an increasing amount of 'cold chiselling' was done; in the hands of a skilled craftsman, however, this did not detract from the quality of a sculpture. In recent years R. Nagaswamy, Director of the Tamil Nadu State Department of Archaeology, has brought to light a large number of unknown bronzes of the early Chola period, several being firmly dated by inscriptions. These new discoveries have necessitated a revision in the dating of South Indian bronzes, many of which are now found to be of an earlier date than hitherto suspected.

Karnataka Sculptures

A group of Jain stone images in the Simon collection come from the Karnataka region which, in ancient days, was a stronghold of the Jain faith. The site of Sravana Belgola, to this day a major pilgrimage spot for Jains, appears to have been a Jain centre from the centuries before Christ. Mahavira, the founder of the Jain faith, lived in the sixth century BC. He did not propound a theology and never claimed to be divine, proclaiming only to have discovered a path to salvation. He was described as a tirthankara (one who has crossed over to the other shore). As the centuries passed, it became a tenet of Jainism that Mahavira had been the last of a set of twenty-four tirthankaras. One of the most widely worshipped of these holy beings is Parsvanatha, the twenty-third in the line, who is believed to have lived some four hundred years before the historical Mahavira. His emblem is the serpent and artists often represented him, as in Figure 1, with the serpent coiled behind him to serve as a backdrop, and its hood above him as a parasol. Jainism is a religion that stresses asceticism and self-denial, and it is customary to depict these great souls naked and in the upright posture of meditation (*kayotsarga*), in which arms are held straight downwards but not touching the body. The image of Parsvanatha, with its robust body and a gentle smile playing upon its lips, is a fine example of Jain sculpture of the tenth century.

(Fig. 1, *opposite*) Jain saint Parsvanatha
Karnataka, 10th century
Schist
Height 82.5 cm
The Norton Simon Foundation

The Jains believe in a set of twenty-four yakshas and yakshis appointed to serve each tirthankara as attendant spirits, and they are often sculpted upon the slabs that depict their master. Gradually a cult arose around some of these beings, and independent images of them began to be made. During the rule of the later Chalukyan period, such figures were often worshipped as independent deities. The Yaksha and Yakshi pair in Figure 2, though not monumental in size, have all the characteristics of cult images. Seated majestically in the position of ease (*lalitasana*), richly adorned and wearing a crown, their commanding presence and serenity of expression are befitting to deities. Their attributes of a flower and a fruit are, however, too generalized to identify them specifically. The images probably date from *c*. 800, before the emergence of a full-fledged Jain cult of yakshis.

Carved in the mid twelfth century when the exuberant style of the Hoysala artists of Karnataka was at its peak, the stone image of Krishna (Fig. 3) portrays him as the flute-playing enchanter who captured the hearts of the cowherd girls. Gracefully poised with one leg crossed casually in front of the other, this large sculpture must have adorned a major temple in the kingdom. It is a striking example of the Hoysala style, in which sculptors specialized in manipulating stone and playing with its tactile qualities to produce an incredible intricacy of surface detail. The exact contour of each gem on Krishna's girdle, details of the ornaments and crown, the texture of his sacred thread and garments absorbed the artist's attention. Equally important to him was the treatment of the leafy bower above the god, where the stone is cut through to produce a trellis-like effect. This concern with detail was extended to the little vignettes that flank Krishna, and to the cows, cowherds and women who flock to listen to Krishna's flute and submit to its enchantment.

(Fig. 2) Jain Yaksha and Yakshi
Karnataka, 9th century
Schist
Heights 69.8 cm, 69.2 cm
The Norton Simon Foundation

(Fig. 3, *opposite*) Krishna as the flute-player
Karnataka, *c*. 1150
Schist
Height 160 cm
The Norton Simon Foundation

Tamil Nadu Sculptures

From the region of Tamil Nadu are two imposing granite sculptures, one representing the sun god Surya (Fig. 4) and the other Vishnu (Fig. 5). Surya holds a lotus bud in each hand and Vishnu exhibits the wheel, conch shell and the gesture of protection. These images of monumental stature have not been detached completely from the block of stone from which they were carved; placed in niches of temples, they were never intended to be viewed from the rear. Their impassive faces, frontality and somewhat static poses reaffirm their power and divinity. Stylistically they show affinities with sculptures from the Madras region, known in ancient time as Tondai-mandalam, which was the centre of Pallava activity. They appear to belong to temples constructed towards the end of Pallava rule, perhaps during the reign of the last Pallava ruler Aparajita (885-903). There is much scholarly debate over the terminology to be used to label South Indian sculptures that date to the second half of the ninth century, since at that time Pallava and Chola rule overlapped for a period of nearly fifty years. Nevertheless these two sculptures may be assigned to the final years of the Pallava dynasty.

(Fig. 4) Surya
Tamil Nadu, *c.* 990
Granite
Height 148.6 cm
The Norton Simon Foundation

(Fig. 5) Vishnu
Tamil Nadu, *c.* 900
Granite
Height 161.2 cm
The Norton Simon Foundation

While the Pallavas are known for their finesse in stone carving, the casting of metal icons was not a developed art with them, and the few bronzes they produced are diminutive in size, rarely more than twenty centimetres in height. The advent of Chola rule saw a remarkable efflorescence in the production of bronze sculptures of a high aesthetic quality which, as a rule, measure approximately ninety centimetres in height. There appears to have been a dramatic increase in temple ceremonies, and the introduction of a series of rituals that had to be performed at frequent intervals. All these rites revolved around portable bronze images of deities, rather than the immovable god enshrined in the sanctum. The Chola bronze casters responded to the need for such images, producing sculptures, with their subtlety of naturalistic modelling and fluent outline of form, that are among the most admired works of Indian art. Chola bronzes are particularly attractive in Western eyes; it was a Chola bronze of dancing Siva that captured the imagination of the French sculptor Auguste Rodin (1840-1917). He spoke of it as the perfect embodiment of rhythmic movement, proclaimed its elegance and grace, its softness and power, and ended with the remark that words were inadequate to express the beauty of the image.

Chola Bronzes: the Tenth Century

The earliest South Indian bronze in the Simon collection is a sinuously elegant sculpture of Siva as Tripurantaka (Destroyer of Tripura; Fig. 6), the heroic aspect in which the god, with a single arrow, destroyed the forts of three demons. Noteworthy for its extraordinary fluidity of outline, the image belongs to the early years of the tenth century. With one leg flexed, the slender god stands in a twice-bent (*dvibhanga*) pose with torso leaning to his right to culminate in an out-thrust hip, and limbs below poised in the opposite direction; his outstretched hands once held a bow and arrow. The handsome image is equally enthralling when seen from the rear. Two long necklaces grace Siva's chest and a serpent rears above his right shoulder. His armlets are knotted with a single tie, a waist band (*kati sutra*) circles his narrow torso and his lower garment, which moulds his limbs, has a triangular splay at the back. His tall

matted locks display the crescent moon, and a small, elegant lotus-petalled halo completes the image. This animated piece is a masterpiece of early Chola art (no more than a dozen bronzes from this early period are known), and it is certainly one of the most significant pieces in the collection.

From recorded evidence, we know that one of the greatest patrons of tenth-century Chola art was a woman, Queen Sembiyan Mahadevi, who was the daughter-in-law of King Parantaka. Sembiyan's husband, Gandaraditya, died after ruling the Chola kingdom for a mere eight years, and the young widow, not yet thirty years old, decided to devote her life to piety and temple art. Over a period of sixty years (941-1006), she built numerous stone temples, commissioned bronze sculptures, made endowments of land and money for temple maintenance and donated lavish jewellery to adorn the deities. A majestic bronze of the goddess Parvati (Fig. 7), consort of Siva, whose dignified stance and

(Fig. 6, *left*) Siva as Tripurantaka
Tamil Nadu, *c.* 920
Bronze
Height 77.5 cm
The Norton Simon Foundation

(Fig. 7) Parvati
Tamil Nadu, *c.* 970
Bronze
Height 76.1 cm
The Norton Simon Foundation

withdrawn expression evoke awe and respect, was produced by the bronze workshop of Queen Sembiyan. The planes of her body are finely modelled and the treatment of the high breasts, exceedingly slender waist and smoothly rounded stomach is characteristic of the finest work of the early Chola period. The sharply detailed jewellery, including the necklace (*channavira*) which rests upon her shoulders and encircles her breasts, the armlets with a knotted tie and the girdle placed low on her hips, serve to emphasize the soft planes of the body. The sensitive interpretation of this svelte crowned figure is similar to that of

Somaskanda
Bronze
South India: Chola Period

a group of bronzes dated to 970 from a temple at Konerirajapuram; the temple was a monument erected by the queen in memory of her husband.

A joyous Somaskanda group of Siva and Parvati (Fig. 8) seated at ease with their infant son Skanda standing between them comes from the same workshop. The goddess is a seated replica of the standing Parvati in Figure 7, and the god is akin in style. The pattern of the fabric that drapes both god and goddess — successive bands of circles, triangles and a scroll — is identical to that seen on several dated images of Queen Sembiyan Mahadevi, including the group from Konerirajapuram. This particular design appears to be the hall-mark, so to speak, of one particular bronze master.

Although the famous Sivapuram Nataraja is now in India, the Simon collection has two other images of Nataraja, one of which dates from the tenth century (Fig. 9). Creating a harmonious, balanced composition, Siva stands on his right foot, with

his left leg raised in dance, and the graceful gesture of his left hand follows the direction of the leg. The supple figure is imbued with a rhythmic sense of movement further emphasized by the whirling scarf around his waist and the locks of hair splayed out with the movement of dance. To the seventh-century Saiva saint, Appar, the form is one of such great beauty that he considered even rebirth in this world was to be welcomed provided one could gaze upon the dancing Siva.

If one may see
his arched eyebrows —
the gentle smile
upon his lips of *kovai* red —
his matted locks
of reddish hue —
the milk-white ash
upon his coral form —
if one may but see
the beauty of his lifted foot
of golden glow
then indeed
one would wish for human birth
upon this earth.

(Fig. 8) Siva and Parvati with Skanda
Tamil Nadu, *c.* 970
Bronze
Height 58.4 cm
The Norton Simon Foundation

The philosophical concept behind the visualization of Siva dancing to destroy and yet re-create the world was formulated by the end of the ninth century, and both bronze and stone images of the god in this pose were introduced shortly afterwards. The gentle sensuousness of modelling apparent in this slender figure of Siva Nataraja dancing the dance of bliss (*ananda tandava*), belongs to the very end of the tenth century.

South Indian bronzes, admired today as works of art, were originally created solely as icons of worship to be carried ceremonially through the temple and the adjoining areas of a town. The lugs and holes on the base of all South Indian bronzes were to ensure that poles could be inserted through them to facilitate their transportation on the shoulders of bearers.

(Fig. 9) Siva Nataraja
Tamil Nadu, *c.* 990
Bronze
Height 80.7 cm
The Norton Simon Foundation

An inscription of Queen Sembiyan Mahadevi gives us details of the rituals connected with these bronze temple images. Bronzes were anointed with sandalwood paste and bathed with water from the sacred River Kaveri; they were draped with special dyed cloth and adorned with garlands; they were carried in processions with canopies held above them; they received offerings of food, incense and lamps; and within the temple precincts, watchmen were appointed to guard them. The practice of clothing, garlanding and ornamenting bronze images, so much so that it is all but impossible to appreciate their beauty, is not a recent innovation; rather it is the continuation of a custom more than a thousand years old. A visit to a South Indian temple makes one sharply aware of the fact that a true appreciation of a bronze image is possible only in a museum where it stands divested of its customary paraphernalia and where one may feast one's eyes on the graceful contours of a clothed (in bronze) yet 'unclothed' figure. The Norton Simon bronzes are, in addition, displayed in such a manner that one may walk right round them and fully appreciate their line and form.

Two Great Emperors: Eleventh-century Chola Bronzes

The most renowned period of South Indian history is the eleventh century when two great emperors, father and son, were responsible for making the Chola empire into the dominant political force in India. Rajaraja ('King of Kings') and Rajendra ('Indra

42

among Kings') extended the boundaries of the empire beyond South India to Sri Lanka and the Maldive islands, and temporarily even took over parts of the Sailendra kingdom of Java. They maintained diplomatic relations with various countries including China. These two dynamic monarchs shaped the artistic activity of their times, constructing monumental stone temples adorned with carvings and paintings, and commissioning some of the most evocative of Chola bronzes.

Many of the Simon bronzes belong to the eleventh century when the art of bronze-casting reached a peak in South India. Dating from the early years of the century, the majestic and

authoritative image of Siva as rider of the bull, with one arm bent to rest upon the now-missing animal and accompanied by his consort, strikes a graceful posture (Fig. 10). A comparison of the Simon Siva with the famous Siva image in the Tanjore Art Gallery, dated by inscription to the year 1011, reveals their contemporaneity. The figures share the broad shoulders and somewhat solid form that are characteristic of the workshop of the great Chola emperor Rajaraja; the details of decoration and ornament are also similar. Portraits of the emperor painted in the Great Temple at Tanjore depict him as a broad-shouldered, sturdy and pragmatic

(Fig. 10) Siva as rider of the bull and Parvati
Tamil Nadu, *c.* 1000
Bronze
Heights 100.4 cm, 87.6 cm
The Norton Simon Foundation

figure with matted locks piled high upon his head, the coiffure of his favourite deity Siva. It is intriguing to ponder the extent to which god and emperor were identified in the minds of artists who produced an image such as this.

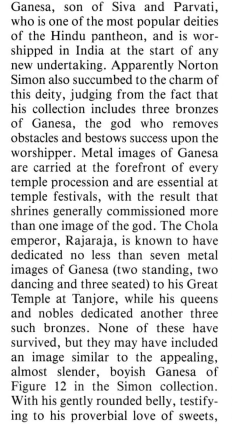

(Fig. 11, *above*) Siva as Bhairava
Tamil Nadu, *c.* 1015
Bronze
Height 22.8 cm
The Norton Simon Foundation

(Fig. 12) Ganesa
Tamil Nadu, early 11th century
Bronze
Height 40.6 cm
The Norton Simon Foundation

A powerful sculpture of Siva in his fierce aspect of Bhairava (Fig. 11) displays majestic presence despite its small size. Standing erect in a rigorous frontal pose, the god wears a sacred thread composed of human skulls strung together and holds a skull bowl in one hand. His stern expression, flaming halo and the fangs protruding from his closed lips combine to make him a formidable figure. Adorned with jewellery, his only garment is a snake loosely knotted around his loins, which barely covers him. One is reminded of a verse by Saint Sambandar that comments on Siva's eccentric mode of dress:

With perfect touch
he tied upon his waist
the angry hissing serpent
to serve in place
of loin cloth —
as only he could do.

Iconographic simplicity and the rare occurrence of bizarre figures are some of the reasons for the appeal of Chola bronzes to Western connoisseurs. An exception is the elephant-headed god Ganesa, son of Siva and Parvati, who is one of the most popular deities of the Hindu pantheon, and is worshipped in India at the start of any new undertaking. Apparently Norton Simon also succumbed to the charm of this deity, judging from the fact that his collection includes three bronzes of Ganesa, the god who removes obstacles and bestows success upon the worshipper. Metal images of Ganesa are carried at the forefront of every temple procession and are essential at temple festivals, with the result that shrines generally commissioned more than one image of the god. The Chola emperor, Rajaraja, is known to have dedicated no less than seven metal images of Ganesa (two standing, two dancing and three seated) to his Great Temple at Tanjore, while his queens and nobles dedicated another three such bronzes. None of these have survived, but they may have included an image similar to the appealing, almost slender, boyish Ganesa of Figure 12 in the Simon collection. With his gently rounded belly, testifying to his proverbial love of sweets,

the crowned Ganesa holds a flat cake in one left hand and a rosary, now broken, in the other, while his right hands hold an axe and a tusk.

The concentration of bronzes of Saiva affiliation may have given the reader the impression, quite rightly, that the worship of Siva was of prime importance in South India. However, Vishnu temples certainly existed, and they possessed their own set of bronze sculptures. An example of these is an icon of Vishnu (Fig. 13) standing rigidly in a frontal pose called *samabhanga*, the traditional mode for the god. This image is an impressive realization that may be compared for its treatment of form and decorative details with the eleventh-century Vishnu in the Tanjore Art Gallery. The Tanjore image forms part of a group of four depicting the marriage of Siva and Parvati. The wheel in the Simon Vishnu has its edge facing the viewer, while in the Tanjore Vishnu the full circle is visible. The full frontal view of the wheel is generally taken to be a later feature and the edge-on view earlier. However, the differing treat-

ment on two contemporaneous images emphasizes the danger of using single decorative elements to date sculptures.

Another popular Vaishnava commission is a group celebrating the god Rama, hero of the *Ramayana*, together with his wife Sita, brother Lakshmana and the monkey god Hanuman, who played a vital role in the story. A youthful, almost adolescent male image (Fig. 14), gracefully poised to hold bow and arrow in his hands, appears to represent the young Lakshmana who accompanied his elder brother Rama into exile in the forest. Although Lakshmana is usually depicted as a mature prince, the artist of the Simon piece has chosen to give him a youthful appearance that is, in fact, more appropriate to the original story.

Most of the sculptures considered so far were made for Hindu temples, and a few were made for Jain shrines. Buddhism too was extremely popular in South India until the seventh century when a group of Hindu saints worked to establish the supremacy of the Hindu faith. While Buddhism slowly

disappeared, an exceptionally strong Buddhist centre continued to exist at the coastal town of Nagapattinam until the seventeenth century. During the reign of Emperor Rajaraja, a mission from the Sailendra king of Java obtained permission to build a major monastery at Nagapattinam, and Rajaraja granted them a village for the maintenance and upkeep of the monastery. Another mission was similarly received during the reign of Kulottunga I. It is clear that despite the personal commitment of the Chola emperors to the worship of Siva, they did not undermine the authority of the Buddhists at Nagapattinam.

The Simon collection possesses two fine Nagapattinam sculptures of the Buddha, one of stone and the other of bronze (see last illustration in Pratapaditya Pal's article on the Norton Simon Museum). The granite image depicts the Buddha seated in meditation and totally absorbed in self-enquiry. The monastic robe is draped so as to leave his right shoulder bare, with the band of the garment returning over his left shoulder in a manner

(Fig. 13, *left*) Vishnu
Tamil Nadu, early 11th century
Bronze
Height 48.5 cm
The Norton Simon Foundation

(Fig. 14) Lakshmana
Tamil Nadu, 11th century
Bronze
Height 77.5 cm
The Norton Simon Foundation

typical of South Indian Buddhist images. Also characteristic of this region is the flame that emerges from the top of the Buddha's head, representing true knowledge that is said to hover above the Buddha's head like a flame. The solid, columnar mass of the body is impressive in its strength and vigour, and the image, with its serene, elegant expression, may indeed have been carved for one of the royal Sailendra monasteries. The impressive standing bronze Buddha from Nagapattinam displays the alternative though less frequent mode of drapery, in which the monastic robe covers both shoulders. The outer edge of the robe has the scalloped folds seen frequently from the twelfth century onwards.

45

Chola Bronzes: the Twelfth Century

The high artistic standard of bronze-casting, and indeed of temple architecture and stone sculpture, that was achieved in the eleventh century was maintained into the twelfth century, despite a change in the lineage of the Chola emperors. When the last of the sons of Emperor Rajendra died without an heir, a young prince of the eastern Chalukya kingdom, to the north of Chola territory, assumed the vacant Chola throne. This prince was, in fact, a half-grandson of Emperor Rajendra since both his mother and grandmother were Chola princesses. He took the ambitious title of Kulottunga ('Star of the Dynasty'), thus reaffirming his claim to Chola ancestry. Although he introduced into Chola art certain features characteristic of the temples of his Chalukyan homeland, the new emperor and his successors of the twelfth century continued to provide patronage to Chola artists. Bronze casters, in particular, produced sculptures in the typical Chola style, as is evident from the restrained elegance and majestic dignity of Siva (Fig. 15) playing upon the musical instrument

known as the *vina*. With two front hands flexed in the gesture of plucking the instrument's strings, and two rear hands holding an axe and an antelope, Siva's withdrawn countenance expresses his absorption in the music he is producing. Another fine bronze represents the dancing child Krishna (Fig. 16), one of the most popular figures with the artist and Vishnu devotee alike. In the ninth century, the Vaishnava poet-saint Periyalvar composed a set of fifty poems dedicated to every aspect of the infant Krishna's growth into childhood. Individual poems celebrate the cutting of Krishna's first tooth, his first steps, clapping his hands, protesting over a bath, uttering his first lisping words and the like. These poems further popularized the enchantment and appeal of the antics of the child Krishna. In this example the artist of the Krishna image has portrayed a winsome child gracefully poised in dance, with one leg raised and one hand outstretched in a gesture of dance, while the other hand promises protection to the devotee. Like the image of Siva with the *vina*, this bronze, with its harmoniously balanced form, reflects the maintenance of a high point in metal working.

(Fig. 15, *left*) Siva as player of *vina*
Tamil Nadu, 12th century
Bronze
Height 57.5 cm
The Norton Simon Foundation

(Fig. 16) Dancing Krishna
Tamil Nadu, 12th century
Bronze
Height 52.7 cm
The Norton Simon Foundation

Vijayanagar Bronzes: Fifteenth Century

When Chola rule ended in the thirteenth century, a period of political turmoil followed during which the Muslims invaded and occupied parts of erstwhile Chola territory. The final quarter of the fourteenth century saw the overthrow of Muslim supremacy and the emergence of the last great empire of South India, the Hindu Vijayanagar (City of Victory) dynasty. Under their patronage, temples destroyed by the Muslims were rebuilt, several new shrines were constructed, and large numbers of broken bronzes were replaced by newly cast images. The fifteenth century

46

witnessed an unusually animated phase of artistic activity, and two fine bronzes in the Simon collection were produced at this time. One of these is an aesthetically satisfying and utterly charming bronze of the child saint, Sambandar (Fig. 17), an ardent worshipper of the god Siva. Sambandar is a historical personage who lived in the seventh century and composed four thousand verses which form part of the Sacred Canon chanted in Saiva temples of South India. The child often approached Siva using the 'lover-beloved' mode, and assuming the role of a love-sick maiden.

Sambandar is depicted as a child because he alone among the saints achieved this elevated status at an early age, and 'died' into grace at the age of sixteen. The bronze depicts a plump, naked child wearing ornaments, with an empty cup in one hand and the index finger of the other pointing upwards. The reason for this gesture lies in the story of the child saint. Left on the steps of the temple tank while his father had a ritual dip, the hungry three-year-old child began crying, and the goddess Parvati is said to have given him a cup of divine milk. When Sambandar's father emerged from his bath, he found his son playing contentedly with an empty golden cup, while trickles of milk ran down his chin. When asked who had given him the milk, the child pointed upwards to the temple tower, where there was an image of the goddess Parvati seated beside Siva. The artist has taken this crucial moment from the story of Sambandar and translated it into effective visual imagery.

Also of fifteenth-century date is a group representing the god Aiyanar flanked by his two consorts Puranai and Pudgalai (Fig. 18). Aiyanar is a deity of considerable antiquity; as a village god he finds mention in the inscriptions of the Chola king, Rajaraja, and he continues to be a popular deity to this day. Every village has a shrine to Aiyanar who is visualized as a guardian deity, nightly patrolling the village, mounted on a ghostly steed. His simple clay shrine is readily recognized by the multitudes of clay horses in front of it, all offerings from his devotees, to serve as the steeds upon which to make his nightly rounds. This folk deity is among the few village gods to be incorporated into the classical Hindu pantheon and he was represented in bronze in the classical style.

The Simon group is rather rare in that it includes two wives of Aiyanar. In the process of adoption into the Hindu pantheon Aiyanar seems to have been modelled closer to the figure of Siva than Vishnu, though theoretically he is the son of both. Like Siva he has a crown of matted hair and an ascetic's band supporting his left leg, but otherwise he has a regal posture and a commanding presence. His rural past is preserved in the shepherd's crook in his right hand.

(Fig. 17, *left*) Sambandar
Tamil Nadu, 15th century
Bronze
Height 24.1 cm
The Norton Simon Foundation

(Fig. 18) Aiyanar and his consorts
Tamil Nadu, 15th century
Bronze
Height 25.6 cm
The Norton Simon Foundation

Although proportionately almost child-like, his two wives are depicted as simple but charming village girls rather than the regal goddesses associated with Siva or Vishnu.

The Norton Simon Museum today possesses more than fifty South Indian sculptures, making it one of the most extensive collections of this material outside India. Clearly the strength of the collection lies in the extraordinary range of Chola bronzes of which Norton Simon is exceptionally fond. To enjoy their sensuous immediacy, there is no need to have an intimate knowledge of Indian philosophy or iconography; this is an art which communicates with the viewer directly, in terms of an overt physical imagination.

Vidya Dehejia is Associate Professor, Department of Art History, Columbia University, New York.

Suggested further reading

Douglas Barrett, *Early Cola Bronzes*, Bombay, 1965.

R. Nagaswamy, *Masterpieces of Early South Indian Bronzes*, New Delhi, 1983.

C. Sivaramamurti, *South Indian Bronzes*, New Delhi, 1963.

Art from the Himalayas

Robert E. Fisher

The world's largest mountain ranges, the Himalayas, stretch from Afghanistan in the west to Burma and China in the east. For millennia this vast landmass, with some of the most inhospitable and inaccessible regions of the world, has nevertheless sustained several nations and a variety of cultures. The ethnic and cultural diversity of the area is also reflected in the arts. The Himalayan cultural traditions have been dominated largely by three distinct geographical regions, Kashmir, Nepal and Tibet. Of these, Kashmir and Nepal are situated in remarkably small valleys but their cultural influence has spread over an area totally disproportionate to their size. Tibet, on the other hand, is a vast country which has for the past millennium remained a dominant cultural force, particularly among the peoples of Mongolian origin from the Indus River in the west to the Brahmaputra and beyond in the east.

The two major religions that have inspired much of the art in the Himalayas are Hinduism and Buddhism, both of which originated in the Indian subcontinent. Most Kashmiris today are Muslims but prior to the fourteenth century the area was a bastion of both Hindu and Buddhist faith and learning. Nepal is predominantly Hindu but has a substantial Buddhist population in the Kathmandu Valley as well as in the more mountainous regions of the country. Tibet, on the other hand, has since the eighth century remained primarily a Buddhist country. All these areas share the characteristic of being cultures that developed out of the Indian tradition, and yet have evolved distinct features, depending upon the confines of their mountainous borders and the amount of influence exerted by other cultures, particularly those using these areas as an avenue between the Indian subcontinent and the vastness of Central Asia and China. Over the centuries each developed distinctive artistic traditions, at times influenced by one another, such as the Kashmiri impact upon the art of Ladakh and Tibet, but each also absorbed influences from outside the region, such as the Chinese impact upon the art of Tibet.

The Simon collection includes sculptures and paintings from Kashmir, Nepal and Tibet, both Hindu and Buddhist, mostly the latter. The objects were acquired principally for their aesthetic merits rather than their iconographic interest. In contrast to Simon's Indian and Southeast Asian collections, which comprise both stone and metal sculptures, the Himalayan group includes only the latter. However, while the greater part of his Asian collection is confined to sculptures, there are two outstanding examples of paintings from Nepal and a colossal appliqué hanging from Tibet. This hanging is so large that no single wall in the museum is big enough to display it.

The general term 'bronze' is used throughout but Himalayan artists favoured alloys with greater amounts of copper and brass. In the case of Tibetan and Nepalese metal images, copper or brass would be more accurate and brass is clearly the correct designation for Kashmiri metalworks. The brass content of Kashmiri images is so high that they often appear to be gilded, but this process, so popular in metal casting in most of Asia, is not found in Kashmir. In addition, Kashmiri metal images often include inlay, usually silver for the eyes and copper for the lips. Other portions may also be enriched by these additions, most notably the inlaid cushion on the eighth-century seated Buddha image (Figs 1 and 1a). The preference for brass and inlay make Kashmiri metal sculptures unique to the Indian subcontinent. Nepalese metal images are notable for their use of semi-precious stones, found in crowns and as part of the often elaborate jewellery worn by the various deities. Like Tibetan metal images, the Nepalese figures are often gilded but when left alone they reveal a reddish surface, due to their high copper content. Tibetans are especially fond of gilding their figures and, even more so than the Nepalese, they encrust their images with semi-precious stones, the turquoise being especially popular.

Kashmir

Among the finest Himalayan pieces in the Simon collection are the group of bronzes from Kashmir. Throughout most of the first millennium AD Kashmir enjoyed a special prestige among Buddhists and Hindus alike as a centre of learning and this religious and philosophical activity was matched by an artistic tradition of notable stature within the broad spectrum of South Asian culture. Although some Kashmiri bronze and stone images are assigned dates as early as the fifth century, clearly revealing their Gupta (c. 320-600) and Gandharan sources, not until the eighth century, during the Karkota dynasty (late 7th-c. 855), did the fully developed style emerge, nowhere better illustrated than in the seated Buddha in Figures 1, 1a and cover.

This masterpiece of Kashmiri bronze casting of the Buddha, seated on top of a three-tiered mountain, is the crown jewel of Himalayan art in the Simon collection and the most sumptuous of all of the Kashmiri bronzes. With its elaborate pedestal, inlaid cushion and the elegant form of the figure, it is a *tour de force* among Kashmiri metal sculptures. Especially effective is the progression through the three parts, beginning with the animal realm along the bottom, then moving up to the human world, which is alloted twice the space, and finally the celestial realm above, more than three times the size of the human domain. The contrast is made more dramatic by the actions and poses of the figures. The animals are playful, as are the two humans in the cave, while the donors and their two attendants, at either end of the second level, are represented in poses of homage, repeated by the two identical bodhisattvas on either side.

(Fig. 1) Buddhist altarpiece
Kashmir, 8th century
Brass with copper and silver inlay
Height 33.6 cm
The Norton Simon Foundation

(Fig. 1a) Base of Buddhist altarpiece in Figure 1

(Fig. 2, *above*) Buddha
Kashmir, *c.* 800
Brass
Height 36.8 cm
The Norton Simon Foundation

(Fig. 3) Manjusri
Kashmir, 9th century
Brass
Height 29.8 cm
The Norton Simon Foundation

The figure of the Buddha, perched on the richly decorated cushion with his right hand in the gesture representing enlightenment, appears to float above the smaller, mundane world below, completing a composition that is a remarkable expression of religious hierarchy and aesthetic unity.

Several details are also worthy of note, reflecting the rich cultural mixture of the eighth century, Kashmir's greatest period of international activity. The silver and copper inlaid cushion follows a style well-known among contemporaneous Sassanian bronzes and Central Asian textiles as do the garments and jewellery worn by the two donor figures. The playful, naturalistic animals likewise may also derive from outside sources, perhaps from Tang (618-907) China, while the stylized mountains continue a type from within India, as seen among the wall paintings at Ajanta. The consummate casting skill, inlay work and refined details support the view that this masterpiece came from a royal atelier, perhaps one of the major eighth-century Karkota kings, either Jayapida (r. end of eighth century) or even the most famous of all Kashmiri monarchs, Lalitaditya (r. *c.* 725-56).

A second seated Buddha figure in the collection (Fig. 2), less elaborate than the altarpiece, exhibits many of the same stylistic features and is historically an important bronze. The inscription along the base, as translated by Pran Gopal Paul, informs us:

Success: This is the pious gift of the Buddhist monk Ratnacitta. [Whatever merit there is in the act] let it be for the attainment of supreme knowledge of the parents, together with preceptors and teachers, together with all sentient beings. The year 70, the 8th day of the bright half of the month Asvayuja.

Although the date is interpreted by Paul as corresponding to 694, stylistically the figure is closer to works of the eighth century and more correctly should be given a date a century later. Especially notable is the facial treatment, the fleshy lips and chin, as well as the inlaid, narrow, downturned eyes and the large auspicious mark on the forehead (*urna*), all commonly found among bronzes of the late eighth to early ninth century. Although derivative of the previous work, it is a more 'mannered' figure with adequate but dry modelling. The Buddha here is depicted as a teacher and he may represent either Buddha Sakyamuni or Vairochana, one of the transcendental Buddhas.

Like the extraordinary altarpiece with Buddha (Fig. 1), a large bronze depicting Manjusri (Fig. 3), the bodhisattva of wisdom, is thematically unique and aesthetically one of the finest Kashmiri bronzes known. Although not as sumptuous as the Buddha, it is an imposing figure with an attractive, warm patina. This crowned, six-armed standing figure reflects a blending of Buddhist and Hindu iconography as well as the growing influence of esoteric ideas.

The crown and long garland derive from Vaishnava images and the peacock from the Hindu god Kumara. However, the presence of the book and the lotus in the left hands, and the absence of Kumara's six heads and lance clearly identify this image as Manjusri. Especially engaging is the stylishly rendered peacock who looks up adoringly at his master. The details of the bird, dhoti, ornaments and hair of Manjusri are all depicted with great finesse. Also noteworthy is the unusual abundance of jewellery which together with the multiple arms, braids of hair and sweep of the peacock's tail make this an exceptionally lovely figure. This luxuriance of shapes reflects the bodhisattva's identification with Kama, the Hindu god of desire. The elaborate iconography and ornamentation and the rather fleshy body suggest a mid ninth-century date for this unusual figure of Manjusri.

Somewhat later in date and stylistically different is a small but charming bronze depicting the important Vajrayana deity, Vajrasattva (Fig. 4). Adorned as a bodhisattva he sits on a lotus in the classic posture of meditation. The base below the lotus is typically Kashmiri as is the extension

of his knees beyond the circumference of the lotus seat. With his right hand he holds the thunderbolt against his chest and the bell is held in the left hand against his hip. Also typical of Kashmiri figures he has large staring eyes which are made prominent by the silver inlay, with the eyes outlined and eyebrows rendered in black. Despite his static posture the expressive eyes, flying fillets of the tiara, aureole and halo contribute to the liveliness of the composition. The pointed shape of the nimbus and the stylized, summary flame design are characteristic of Buddhist bronzes in Kashmir after the ninth century.

One of the most popular types of Kashmiri bronze sculpture is a particular version of the standing Vishnu (Fig. 5). Whether portrayed with one head or four, these images follow a consistent iconographic pattern. Two of the four hands touch the heads of attendant figures, personifications of Vishnu's emblems, while the other two hands hold the attributes, the lotus and the conch shell. Vishnu wears a long garland that crosses over the shoulders and falls below the knees; between his feet rises the earth goddess, looking in adoration at the deity. Behind

(Fig. 4, *left*) Vajrasattva
Kashmir, *c.* 900
Bronze
Height 23.2 cm
The Norton Simon Foundation

(Fig. 5) Vishnu with attendants
Kashmir, 9th century
Brass with inlay
Height 21 cm
The Norton Simon Foundation

the crowned head is a circular halo. Despite the rubbed surface, typical of Hindu images from continuous worship in the home as compared with Buddhist figures which remain in the monastery, all the essential elements, except for the elaborate crowns, are still visible in this example. This type of Vishnu image originated in Mathura, during the Kushan period (1st-3rd centuries), and became especially popular in Kashmir during the Karkota period.

(Fig. 6, *above*) Vajrapurusha
Nepal, *c.* 1000
Gilt bronze
Height 29.9 cm
The Norton Simon Foundation

(Fig. 7) Ratnapani
Nepal, 1st half 11th century
Gilt bronze
Height 43.2 cm
The Norton Simon Foundation

Nepal

The largest number of Himalayan objects are from the land-locked kingdom of Nepal, located in the small Kathmandu Valley and which still retains its monarchical government. North of this cultural and historical centre rise the world's tallest mountains. Amidst these numerous valleys and peaks are seldom explored areas with monasteries and temples differing little from those in Tibet. About 1700 years ago, North Indian peoples, the Lichchhavis, entered the Kathmandu Valley, beginning a series of dynasties and an artistic tradition that has evolved into a distinctive style, borrowing and yet different from both the Tibetans to the north and the various Indian traditions of the plains below. As might be expected, the earliest Nepalese images are similar to those from India, especially Gupta and Pala (*c.* 750-1150) styles, while later

works, both painting and sculpture, reveal affinities with Tibetan art, for Nepalese artists often worked in Tibet for Tibetan patrons, continuing the traditional artistic and commercial relationships between the two regions. Scholarship of the past quarter century has revealed that Nepalese culture is a remarkable and distinctive element of the Himalayan region and its artistic traditions one of the most dynamic in South Asia.

All of the Simon Nepalese sculptures are bronzes, ranging in date from the tenth to the seventeenth century. Among the earliest is a compelling image known as Vajrapurusha (Fig. 6), originally a subsidiary figure, but in Nepal has become the focus of a cult. This early bronze is an example of a type of Buddhist image that demonstrates the uniqueness of the Nepalese sculptural tradition. The youthful Vajrapurusha is the personification of the divine attribute of

both the Hindu god, Indra, and the Buddhist deity, Vajrapani, with the *vajra* (thunderbolt) clearly visible in this example, emerging from the head. Some of the primary attributes of Indian deities, such as Siva's trident or Vishnu's various emblems, often came to be represented as attendant figures. The influence of Hindu deities can also be seen in his bird-like nose, deriving from Garuda, the eagle-like mount of Vishnu and conqueror of serpents, as well as in the feline skin worn about the waist, associated especially with Siva. The demonic face, plethora of serpents, disposition of the arms and flying scarves, which form an additional halo, point to Nepalese stylistic modifications and to the early development of a separate cult devoted to Vajrapurusha, a practice unknown in India. His angry demeanour and the prominence given to serpents would link this image more to the Buddhist Vajrapani than to Indra, the former

being closely associated with the rain-controlling serpents in Nepal. The gesture of crossed arms is familiar in classical Indian dance and in other contexts is considered a posture of submission, although the attitude of this fiercely proud figure would otherwise belie a submissive role.

The elegant standing bodhisattva images, with their seductive charm, may be regarded as the hallmark of Nepalese figurative sculpture. Unlike most such figures usually representing Avalokiteshvara, Maitreya or Vajrapani, the Simon bodhisattva in Figure 7 depicts Ratnapani, rarely encountered among bodhisattva images. The presence of the flaming jewel (*ratna*) in the left hand, instead of the lotus, clearly identifies him as Ratnapani. The jewel, shown here surrounded by flames, is called a 'wishing jewel' and represents the granting of the devotee's prayers. In Nepal this figural form has remained a classic

type and has been repeatedly adopted to represent various bodhisattvas. Characteristic of Nepalese figures from earlier times, this handsomely proportioned Ratnapani stands securely on a double lotus pedestal and holds the ubiquitous boss symbolizing the fruit of knowledge in his right hand, extended in the gesture of charity. Stylistically he is closely related to the Vajrapurusha both in details, such as the lotus, dhoti or flame halo, and in the overall sensitive, plastic quality.

An especially graceful and elegant figure is the seated Indra (Fig. 8) which, like the Vajrapani, is also characteristic of a Nepalese creation. The king of the Vedic gods is shown in the posture of royal ease, expressing the dignity and majesty of his position. The details of the casting are particularly fine, most notably the facial features, the gesture of the right hand, in the position of discussion or dialogue, and the bound-up hair,

(Fig. 8) Indra
Nepal, 12th century
Gilt bronze
Height 40.9 cm
The Norton Simon Foundation

hidden behind the tall crown in frontal views. Nepalese images of Indra were often represented in this elegant pose, reflecting the lofty, dominant position Indra enjoyed there, unlike his diminished role in India. In fact, Indra's rise in popularity in Nepal largely coincided with his decline in India, about the tenth century. In addition to this posture, images of Indra are notable for the horizontal third eye, as compared with Siva's vertical one and, in Nepal, for the distinctively shaped tiara. Sometimes Indra also holds the thunderbolt, emblem of his mastery over the atmosphere, an attribute also represented as Vajrapurusha, as seen in the earlier image.

(Fig. 9) Buddha
Nepal, 12th century
Gilt bronze
Height 70 cm
The Norton Simon Foundation

(Fig. 10) Buddha
Nepal, 13th century
Gilt bronze
Height 35 cm
The Norton Simon Foundation

(Fig. 11) Tara
Nepal, 14th century
Gilt bronze
Height 88.4 cm
The Norton Simon Foundation

Two similar Nepalese Buddha images (Figs 9 and 10) are among the largest bronzes in the Himalayan collection. Both have retained much of their original gilding and in their simplicity project the serenity and calm associated with images of Sakyamuni. Their poses continue the famous Gupta Sarnath type, created in the fourth century, and their gestures are the most frequently used among Nepalese Buddhas, the standing figure exhibiting the wish-granting gesture with the right hand while the seated Buddha touches the earth with the same hand, symbolizing the moment of enlightenment. During the period they were created they may have represented the Buddha Sakyamuni or two of the transcendental Buddhas of the Vajrayana pantheon, Ratnasambhava and Akshobhya.

Even larger than the two Buddhas is the image in Figure 11, possibly of the Buddhist deity, Tara. Easily the most popular Buddhist goddess in Nepal, Tara is the female counterpart of Avalokiteshvara, sharing his functions, mainly protective, as well as his iconography. The gesture of charity, formed with the right hand, and that of teaching, displayed by the raised left hand, are common to both. Probably a lotus was attached to the left arm as is often found in bronzes of this period. Sumptuously adorned, her jewellery is inset with numerous semi-precious, coloured stones with clear crystals reserved for prominent positions: above the crown, on the forehead and at the centre of the necklace. The jewellery and diaphanous garment accent the goddess' sensuality and the entire image is enhanced by the remarkably intact gilding. Images in this posture were widely used to represent the goddess in both Hindu and Buddhist contexts, but when worshipped alone the figure is usually of Tara.

55

(Fig. 12) Saiva scroll
Nepal, *c*. 1600
Opaque watercolour on cotton
Height 35.5 cm, length 184.2 cm
The Norton Simon Foundation

(Fig. 12a) Detail of Figure 12

Included in the Simon collection of Himalayan art are two types of Nepalese painting, a handscroll (Figs 12 and 12a) and a series of *Ragamala* paintings (Fig. 13). The handscroll is in a horizontal format and consists of more than twenty separate scenes, representing a little-known Saiva myth. The story concerns a human, Vadava who, cursed by Siva's wife, is attacked by sea monsters and finally is shown performing the appropriate religious rite and being redeemed by the elephant-headed god Ganesa. Although several early scenes feature Siva, playing dice with Parvati in one composition and in another carousing with her, the scroll is actually dominated by Ganesa, called Manavinayaka in Nepal, who appears no less than six times. In the detail of Figure 12a, he is shown in the lower right corner as a red, twelve-armed figure dancing on his mount, the rat. Indra is shown riding his white elephant; next to him is the four-armed Kumara, astride his peacock; and in the panel below are Brahma, riding his white gander and Vishnu, mounted upon his vehicle, the bird-man Garuda. Collectively, these

Hindu deities are unable to lift the curse placed upon the human Vadava until he performs the sacred rite to Manavinayaka, thereby freeing himself from his troubles and illustrating the greater power of this popular Nepalese god.

This scroll belongs to the tradition of narrative or didactic painting, although most scenes are dominated by singular images of the various gods and goddesses. Such scrolls clearly derive from the older illuminated manuscript tradition, but they rarely

exploit their increased pictorial·spaces, with most compartments containing but one or two figures. The emphasis is on rich colours and decorative backgrounds with simple forms, rather than pictorial details or narrative subtleties. Many of these types of narrative scrolls were utilized by itinerant storytellers as a visual aid, but this version was made to commemorate a particular religious rite and was thus kept rolled up, except for special occasions. The lively, florid style, with vibrant colours and busily

56

patterned backgrounds, emerged late in the sixteenth century. Although the figures had become stylized, the decorative, vegetal backgrounds, mixing naturalism and stylization, made works from this period among the most successful in Nepalese painting.

After about 1625 Nepalese artists moved away from this dynamic style and adopted the Mughal-Rajput tradition of contemporary India. This new mode is best represented by the *Ragamala* series (Fig. 13) in the Simon collection, which has been called the most important Nepalese secular painting known. This remarkable series consists of separate folios illustrating each of the thirty-six musical modes, called *ragas* and *raginis*. Each subject is enclosed within a tri-lobed frame with lotus petals along the bottom and written interpretation of the musical mode along the top. The intense colours and fine drawing derive from Indian Rajput styles, well assimilated in Nepal by the mid-seventeenth century. In the example illustrated in Figure 13, the *Bhairava ragini*, a maiden is shown in profile, holding cymbals during worship before an altar to Siva, whose flower-adorned linga floats in front of her. The scintillating colours of her garment and the white of the linga are dramatically accentuated by the deep black background; this painting is one of the most visually stunning of the series. As has been suggested, the entire series was probably painted for a royal patron. Several rulers in the Nepali kingdom of the period were interested in music.

(Fig. 13) *Bhairava ragini*, from a *Ragamala* series
Nepal, *c.* 1650
Opaque watercolour on paper
Height 17.8 cm, width 14 cm
The Norton Simon Foundation

(Fig. 14) Jambhala
Tibet, 13th-14th century
Bronze
Height 21 cm
The Norton Simon Foundation

Tibet

To Westerners, the most fascinating of the Himalayan cultures is Tibet. With the Chinese takeover, complete in 1965, fleeing Tibetans carried out numerous images, texts and paintings, including those created in neighbouring Kashmir and Nepal, which for centuries had been reverently preserved in Tibetan monasteries. As a consequence, with few exceptions, major Western collections of Tibetan art have been formed during the past twenty-five years. Of the three Himalayan regions, Tibet is the least well represented in the collection: Simon has always been attracted to Indian and Southeast Asian sculpture of more monumental scale; secondly, he did not feel that he could form a complete collection of Tibetan art without acquiring the religious paintings known as thankas, and by and large he has not collected Indian or any other

form of Asian paintings. Moreover, he is conscious of the fact that the Los Angeles County Museum of Art already has a comprehensive collection of Nepalese and Tibetan art and unnecessary duplication would serve no purpose. He, therefore, acquired only a few Tibetan objects, two of which are included in this article.

Of the two, the earlier is a bronze (Fig. 14) rendered in a style derived from the Buddhist art of Bihar of the Pala period, which was a primary source of Tibetan art. Most scholars consider such bronzes to have been created in western Tibet but the style may have been more widespread. They usually have a greyish or olive-green patina and are rarely gilded. Like many Buddhist images that derive from Hindu deities, a borrowing process that was part of the never-ending Indian synthesis and absorption among various religions, the source for this Buddhist image of Jambhala (Fig.

14) is the Hindu deity Kubera. Kubera began as the lord of wealth, ruler of the yakshas and later guardian of the northern quarter, and this important figure appears in the Buddhist pantheon little changed from his earlier Hindu form. In this thirteenth or fourteenth-century Tibetan example Jambhala is shown, corpulent like Kubera, in a relaxed posture upon a lotus pedestal. He squeezes the neck of a mongoose (in Hindu versions simply a sack), which spits forth a stream of jewels, appropriate for the god of wealth. In his right hand he holds an artfully peeled lemon, symbol of fertility. Interesting details include the substantial garland of blue lotuses and the delineation of the band around the base, which supports the lotus pedestal.

The second Tibetan work of art is an appliqué hanging (Figs 15 and 15a) of monumental size. Such large hangings were reserved mainly for festivals,

(Fig. 15, *opposite right*)
Maitreya Buddha
Tibet, *c.* 1780
Silk appliqué
Height 6.7 m, width 7.31 m
The Norton Simon Foundation

(Fig. 15a) Detail Figure 15

at which time they would be unfurled and hung from the balconies of the multi-tiered Tibetan temples. Old photographs show the Potala Palace, in Lhasa, resplendent with these giant hangings, often several side by side, while lengthy processions of lamas wind their way below. The excellent condition of the Simon piece is no doubt due in part to its size, which limited it to occasional use.

The subject is a popular one in Buddhist worship. Maitreya, the Buddha-to-be and emblem of the better world to come, is seated on an elaborate lotus throne, making a variation of the traditional Indian Buddhist gesture of teaching. Surrounding Maitreya are five lamas from the Gelukpa (Yellow Hat) sect and, according to the inscription below, the eighth Dalai Lama (1758-1804) with his guru are shown on either side of the main image; the Dalai Lama is the younger man, to the left of Maitreya. Along the bottom are

the guardians of the four quarters, their martial appearance and protective functions enhanced by flaming aureoles. This hanging was probably fabricated during the lifetime of the eighth Dalai Lama, perhaps even for the Potala Palace.

Robert E. Fisher is Professor of Asian Art and Chairman of the Art History Department, University of Redlands, Redlands, California.

Suggested further reading

Pratapaditya Pal, 'Bronzes of Kashmir: Their Sources and Influences', *Journal of the Royal Society of Arts*, vol. CXXI, no. 5207, 1973, pp. 726-49.
———, *The Arts of Nepal: Sculpture*, Leiden, 1974.
———, *Bronzes of Kashmir*, Verlagsanstalt, Graz, 1975.
———, *The Arts of Nepal: Painting*, Leiden, 1978.
———, *Art of Nepal*, Los Angeles, 1985.
Pran Gopal Paul, *Early Sculpture of Kashmir*, The Netherlands, 1986.

Valrae Reynolds et al, *Tibetan Collection*, vol. III, Newark, 1986 (for reference on technique and casting).
Mary Shepherd Slusser, *Nepal Mandala*, 2 vols, New Jersey, 1982.
David Snellgrove and Hugh Richardson, *A Cultural History of Tibet*, New York and Washington, 1986.

Art from Southeast Asia

Pratapaditya Pal

There are 113 works of Southeast Asian art in the Norton Simon collection. The majority are from Thailand and Cambodia (Kampuchea); a very few are from Indonesia, but the three sculptures from Vietnam are among the finest from that country. Most of the sculptures in the collection are in stone and metal and a few in terracotta. Metal sculptures are generally in copper alloy with the exception of five spectacular gold plaques from Thailand. The collection also includes large groups of bronze drums and Ban Chiang pottery from Thailand, which are not discussed in this article. The sculptures selected here are intended to reflect both the variety and quality of the collection, though like all private collections, it has its limitations. Compared to the Indian collection, the material from Southeast Asia is less comprehensive but no less spectacular. While almost ignoring Indonesia and Burma, Simon has confined himself to the early material from Thailand, but the group from Cambodia is stylistically more diverse.

The earliest objects are from Si Tep (Sri Deb) in Thailand, a site that must have been a flourishing centre of the elusive Mon Dvaravati kingdom. An Austroasiatic people, the Mons originally moved south from southern China and established a state in Thailand that is known by its Indian name of Dvaravati. Whatever its antecedents, the kingdom centred around modern Laro (Lopburi), and for roughly four centuries, from the sixth into the tenth, flourished as one of the most influential states in the region. Unfortunately very little information is available about this mysterious kingdom but it certainly played a major role in the transplan-tation of Indian religious ideas and inspired some of the greatest examples of sculpture fashioned by man.

Thailand

A sandstone sculpture (Fig. 1) in the round in the Simon collection is an example that is universally admired. Although the arms are missing, the figure is generally believed to represent the Hindu sun god Surya, chiefly because of his octagonal crown. How the figure must have looked when complete can be ascertained by comparison with a gold plaque representing the moon god Chandra (Fig. 2c), also in the collection.

While it is generally thought that such sculptures were probably inspired by the styles and aesthetics that prevailed in contemporaneous Gupta (*c.* 320-600) India, this particular sixth-century stone from Si Tep clearly demonstrates how original the early Southeast Asian sculptors were, whether in the Mon Dvaravati kingdom or elsewhere. A notable difference is that most Indian figural sculpture is in the form of deep reliefs, whereas the sculptors of Thailand and Cambodia preferred to represent their figures in the round. This is one reason why Thai and Cambodian images are often broken from the legs, as is the case with several examples in the Simon collection, for they were not provided with adequate support at the ankles and the base and therefore became top-heavy. Following Indian practice, Thai and Cambodian sculptors also preferred abstract but sensuous model-ling of the form and yet there are subtle differences. In the art of Mon Dvaravati and pre-Angkor Cambodia, the overt sensuality found in Gupta sculpture is here more restrained and the plastic qualities of the form are given stronger articulation, exemplified in the Surya and most other early sculptures (Figs. 1 and 4) in the collection. Because the figures are depicted in the round and without a backslab, the contours are better defined and the backs naturalistically modelled and finished. Another major difference between the parent and the offspring is the simplicity of the latter; most Thai and Cambodian figures remain uncluttered by ornaments, which were made separately, probably either in gilt metal or real gold and silver, and attached to the images. In the early figures the garments are also very lightly indicated, as in Figure 1, by linear striations rather than in modelled volume. Thus, in the early sculptures of both Thailand and Cambodia one encounters strong and virile forms with restrained vitality and austere elegance, unencumbered by extraneous or ornamental details, characteristics that are reminiscent of ancient Egyptian sculpture and also recur in the best examples of Pallava (4th-9th centuries) and Chola (*c.* 880-1279) art in South India.

(Fig. 1, *opposite*) Surya
Thailand, Si Tep, 6th century
Sandstone
Height 113.6 cm
The Norton Simon Foundation

(Fig. 2) Four gold plaques: a. Buddha triad,
b. bodhisattva, c. Chandra, d. bodhisattva
Thailand, Si Tep, 7th century
Gold repoussé
Heights 5.7 cm, 12 cm, 9.5 cm and 10.8 cm
The Norton Simon Foundation

(Fig. 3) Vishnu with attendant
Thailand, Si Tep, 7th century
Gold repoussé
Height 30.5 cm
The Norton Simon Foundation

Slightly later in date and much
smaller in size than the sandstone Surya
are five gold repoussé plaques (Figs 2
and 3) representing both Hindu and
Buddhist deities. Although belonging to
two different faiths, they are closely
related in style and were probably made
in the same atelier. As has already been
noted, the figure of Chandra (Fig. 2c)
is remarkably akin to the stone Surya.
Iconographically it is also the most
interesting, for the halo behind the
god's head portrays a running hare.
The belief that the marks on the moon
represent a hare goes back to the Vedic
Aryans (*c.* 1500 BC), but rarely, if at
all, does one come across the animal
represented on the halo of Chandra
in India. Thus, this diminutive gold
plaque may preserve memories of an
iconographic tradition that went out of
fashion in India itself.

The large gold plaque of Figure 3
is a charming representation of the
Hindu god Vishnu standing gracefully
on a rectangular pedestal. By his
side is a lotus-bearing dwarf who
also balances the composition, the
dwarf being the personification of
the lotus, an attribute of Vishnu. Both
in iconography and style, this image of
Vishnu is close to Gupta period models,
although the deity is rarely shown
standing in *dehanchement*, as is the
case with the stone Surya. Unlike
Surya, this representation of Vishnu
has been given ornaments, though of
the simple variety, one encounters in
Gupta sculpture. Moreover, the crown
is surmounted by a lotus flower, a
feature commonly found in Gupta
India. However, unlike Gupta Vishnu
images, the garland of flowers is
dispensed with. Instead, a chain is
loosely tied around the hips. The cloud
designs added on either side of the oval
nimbus and the plain pedestal which
has been rendered in perspective are
also unusual. Equally noteworthy is the
manner of representing the feet. In the
case of Chandra both feet are shown

laterally, recalling the mode preferred in early Indian Buddhist art. In this instance, Vishnu's right foot is splayed and rather clumsily modelled, but the left foot is foreshortened more naturalistically, so is the lower right arm. Because of these attempts to create the illusion of depth, both figures seem remarkably plastic.

The three plaques in Figure 2 represent Buddhist deities of the Mahayana rather than the Theravada school, the latter being more prominent in Thailand. The plaque on top (Fig. 2a) shows a triad consisting of Buddha Sakyamuni flanked by Bodhisattva Maitreya on the right and Bodhisattva Samantabhadra on the left; the former bodhisattva can be identified by the stupa and the latter by the wheel. This is an unusual triad in early Buddhist art of Thailand. Each of the other two plaques (Fig. 2b and d) depicts a bodhisattva seated on a lotus and holding a waterpot of the *kundika* variety in the left hand. The right hand shows the clenched fist, an uncommon gesture. If the conical object faintly visible in the front of their matted hair is a stupa then both must be identified with Maitreya.

It is not known whether the group of gold plaques was found together, but they may well have been made in the same workshop. Usually such plaques were inserted in funerary urns with the remains after a body was cremated. In the case of a Buddhist the objects may have been placed in a stupa. Exactly what form the Hindu memorials took cannot be ascertained. Important personages raised temples; the less fortunate may have been content with small shrines.

The four Mon Dvaravati sculptures of Figures 4 to 7 represent the Buddha. The earliest, in Figure 4, is the most damaged, but what remains is a fine example of the type of Buddha image for which the unknown Dvaravati sculptors are justly famous. How the figure would have looked may be determined from the richly patinated bronze Buddha in Figure 5; both hands would have been placed symmetrically forward of the body, forming the gesture of teaching with their slender and sensitively modelled fingers and thumbs.

There is no doubt that the sixth to seventh-century Dvaravati Buddhas were basically modelled on fifth-century Buddha images from important

(Fig. 4) Torso of Buddha
Thailand, Mon Dvaravati, 7th century
Limestone
Height 92.7 cm
The Norton Simon Foundation

workshops such as Sarnath in Uttar Pradesh or other sites in Madhya Pradesh and the Deccan. The simplicity and transparency of the garments that sensuously hug the body, the elegant proportions and the smoothly modelled outlines are characteristics shared by both Gupta and Dvaravati Buddhas. However, most Dvaravati Buddhas stand in an erect manner while the Indian images are generally represented in a swaying posture. The Dvaravati Buddhas also have more elongated and slender bodies, the lower half being often proportionately longer

than the torso, as in the headless stone figure of Figure 4. The feet are often missing in stone examples, but where they survive, such as in the bronze image of Figure 5, they reveal the Dvaravati sculptor's general discomfort in rendering them naturalistically.

(Fig. 5) Buddha
Thailand, Mon Dvaravati, 9th century
Bronze
Height 57.2 cm
The Norton Simon Foundation

(Fig. 6, *right*) Buddha
Thailand, Mon Dvaravati, 9th century
Bronze
Height 14 cm
The Norton Simon Foundation

The most prominent difference between the Dvaravati figures and the Gupta Buddhas occurs in the disposition of the arms. It is extremely rare in Indian art to find both arms represented in the manner, as seen in the bronze Buddha, that became a hallmark of Dvaravati Buddhas. This mode was not adopted for Buddha images in any other contemporary school in Southeast Asia. No satisfactory explanation of this idiosyncratic disposition has yet been suggested, but until the invention of the so-called 'Walking' Buddha type, this posture and double teaching gesture remained the most distinctive iconographic

features of the Buddha image in Thailand.

A third example (Fig. 7) of the Dvaravati Buddha lacks the subtle modelling and sensuous elegance of the seventh-century stone image (Fig. 4) but it is probably the most monumental of all Thai Buddhist sculptures outside the country. When complete the sculpture must have stood almost three metres high. The large cavity between the eyebrows must originally have been filled with a red stone when the figure looked down on pious devotees in a temple. His size may have been awesome, but the benign expression on his face with the touch of a gentle smile must have been comforting. Even among other Indian and Southeast Asian colossi in the Norton Simon Museum, this serene and graceful figure is a commanding presence.

Figure 6 represents a classic example of a seated Dvaravati Buddha in bronze. One of the finest examples of its type, it shows the Buddha seated in the characteristic posture of meditation with his hands placed on his lap. Here

the right shoulder and arm are left undraped; otherwise the figure is of the same basic type as the standing Buddhas. The shoulders are broad and square, but the outline of the torso is prominently curved. The expanding chest and the flat contracting stomach seem to suggest that he is holding his breath. More significant are the shapes and features of the face, which clearly reflect the Mon ethnic type. Although the lips are full and sensuous, the high cheekbones, the wide-open almond-shaped eyes with prominent eyeballs and the continuous, undulating eyebrow across the forehead are characteristic of Mon Dvaravati Buddhas.

(Fig. 7, *opposite*) Buddha
Thailand, Mon Dvaravati, 9th century
Sandstone
Height 223.5 cm
The Norton Simon Foundation

(Fig. 8) Reliquary with eight Buddhas
Thailand, Lopburi, 13th century
Bronze
Height 23.5 cm
The Norton Simon Foundation

Cambodia

From early Cambodia the eighth-century sandstone sculpture (Fig. 9) depicts the conjoint form of the two principal Hindu gods Siva and Vishnu. Known as Harihara in India, this particular manifestation served as the focus of a royal cult in early Cambodia and came to be known as Harihara-Kambujendra ('Harihara, the Lord of Kambuja', Kambuja being the Sanskrit name of the country). In such images the right half always represents Siva and the left half Vishnu. The differences are emphasized here by the incised hair design on Siva's half of the cylindrical crown, representing the god's chignon, and half a third eye on the right side of the forehead. Of the hands and attributes, the only upper left hand that remains holds Vishnu's conchshell.

By comparison the bronze sculpture of Figure 10, also from the same period, has survived flawlessly. Although his emblems are lost, the effigy of the meditating Buddha in his matted hair identifies him as the Bodhisattva Avalokiteshvara. Unlike Harihara, he stands more gracefully and his short sarong is represented with greater volume and articulation, as is the matted hair. The stone sculpture is probably from a site known as Kompong Preah, but the bronze was found in a hoard in a place called Prakon Chai, now in Thailand. The hoard consisted entirely of Buddhist bronzes but it was not found in a Buddhist temple. A probable explanation is that the bronzes were cast in a well-known metropolitan centre somewhere in Cambodia and were possibly being shipped to an important Buddhist monastery when for some unknown reason they were hidden in a temple at Prakon Chai. Whatever the reason is for their presence in an obscure village in Thailand, aesthetically this imposing sculpture, as large as the stone Harihara, is not only one of the finest of the group but epitomizes the technical accomplishment and aesthetic finesse of eighth-century Cambodian

More elaborate and detailed is a bronze reliquary (Fig. 8) whose top is missing. This thirteenth-century octagonal object contains eight niches, each with a large seated Buddha figure. The Buddha figures are characteristic of the Lopburi figural style of the period, whereas the design of the niches with ornate arches and rearing, multi-hooded serpent capitals reflect influences of contemporaneous Khmer aesthetics of neighbouring Cambodia. The large Buddhas are identical; together they symbolize the eight directions, thereby infusing the object with cosmic symbolism. Each Buddha's right hand forms the specifically Buddhist gesture signifying the master's enlightenment at Bodhgaya, when he extended his right hand to touch the earth to witness his repulsion of the attacks of Mara, the Buddhist god of desire. The prominent fold of the raiment down the left shoulder, the conical shape of both the hair and the cranial bump and the flat, abstract modelling of the body are characteristic of Lopburi Buddhas. Each of the serpent capitals is surmounted by two meditating Buddhas, making the total number of Buddhas in this segment of the reliquary twenty-four, probably signifying the concept of thousand Buddhas.

66

metal sculpture.

Early Cambodian sculptures of the fifth to the ninth century generally share the aesthetic norms with Mon Dvaravati sculptures, but there are subtle differences. The stone Harihara, for example, is stylistically more akin to the Si Tep Surya (Fig. 1) than the bodhisattva from Thailand. Again, although they are like two branches of the same tree, the Harihara and the Avalokiteshvara differ in their proportions, plastic qualities, facial features and expressions. The Harihara is a virile figure with majestic bearing and a strongly modelled but suavely elegant body. The Avalokiteshvara is modelled with greater abstraction; it strikes a more graceful posture, exhibits a more pensive expression with rather narrow and half-shut eyes and is physically less overbearing. Nonetheless both sculptures represent the high watermarks of the early Cambodian sculptors' masterly exploration of the ideal sculptural form.

(Fig. 9, *left*) Harihara
Cambodia, Kompong Preah, 8th century
Sandstone
Height 66 cm
The Norton Simon Foundation

(Fig. 10) Avalokiteshvara
Cambodia, from Thailand, Prakon Chai, 8th century
Bronze
Height 91.4 cm
The Norton Simon Foundation

Among the later schools of Cambodian sculpture, the strongest group in the Simon collection are from a site known as Koh Ker. For two decades Koh Ker was the capital of the realm under Jayavarman IV (921-41). In its brief existence as the capital, the site must have witnessed feverish building activity as is evident from the magnificent Prasat Thom royal complex. The sculptors too enjoyed a hectic period of activity producing some of the most colossal sculptures for their patrons. Two such examples, one representing a Vishnu (Fig. 11) and the other a temple guardian (Fig. 12), are among the most imposing sculptures created by unknown master sculptors of Koh Ker. Not only do they reflect a new style in comparison with the two earlier sculptures, but they demonstrate the artists' technical dexterity with the material as well as their sense of the dramatic.

The sinuous contour and refined plasticity of the earlier sculptures are now replaced by a more geometrically conceived form with emphasis on the rectangular shape and a penchant for ponderous volume. The proportions and shapes of the bodies as well as the faces are quite different with a heavy mid-section and straight shoulders supporting a rather small head with a short neck. The square face is now provided with a stylized, sketchy beard and the head adorned with a pyramidal crown distinctive of Cambodian sculptures. The short dhoti is worn like pants and given greater volume with fine chiselling and elegant, stylish pleats that differ notably from one school to another. The predilection for free-standing sculptures continues, as does the inability to carve the legs with confidence. Naturally, inadequate support for such monumental sculptures had disastrous effects on the figures' ability to stand securely for an indefinite period.

(Fig. 12) Temple guardian
Cambodia, Koh Ker, 10th century
Sandstone
Height 156.8 cm
The Norton Simon Foundation

(Fig. 11, *opposite*) Vishnu
Cambodia, Koh Ker, 10th century
Sandstone
Height 183 cm
The Norton Simon Foundation

This is also true of two smaller sculptures (Figs 13 and 14) in the much admired Baphuon style of the eleventh century. As is the case with most Cambodian sculptures, the lower part of the body is proportionately more elongated than the upper. This unnatural elongation is much more noticeable in the male Avalokiteshvara (Fig. 13), because of the short garment, than it is in the female torso (Fig. 14). Otherwise both figures are excellent examples of the Baphuon style which emphasizes the sensuousness of the human body but in an understated manner. Characteristic also of the Cambodian aesthetic tradition and unlike Indian art, the body is left unencumbered with ornaments but lavish attention is paid to the garment which is carved with an astonishing variety of pleats and folds. It should be noted, however, that the volume of the garment is always indicated by narrow vertical incisions in a uniform manner and by a wide ledge around the flaring hips so that the torso seems to emerge from a container. Characteristically, the Cambodian sculptors did not attempt to render diverse textile patterns as did their Indian counterparts.

Where one does encounter the Cambodian sculptors' penchant for exuberant ornamentation is in their architecture. In many instances the vegetal motifs are rendered with such density and floridity that it seems as if the artists wished to capture some of the lushness of the tropical forests around them. An architectural section (Fig. 15) in the Simon collection, which may once have served as a finial to a balustrade, is a typical example of the Cambodian sculptor's virtuosity in combining both plant and animal motifs into a striking design that is at once imposing and elegant. The fantastic serpents are both menacing and yet delightfully whimsical, while the effusive plant motifs, though stylized, have a life of their own.

Some of the greatest examples of Cambodian architecture were created during the twelfth and thirteenth centuries, of which the best known is the Angkor Wat complex. This period,

(Fig. 14) Female torso
Cambodia, Baphuon, 11th century
Sandstone
Height 87.6 cm
The Norton Simon Foundation

(Fig. 13, *opposite*) Avalokiteshvara
Cambodia, Baphuon, 11th century
Sandstone
Height 111.6 cm
The Norton Simon Foundation

(Fig. 15) Architectural finial
Cambodia, Preah Vihear, 11th century
Sandtone
Height 107.7 cm
The Norton Simon Foundation

(Fig. 16, *below*) Lintel with depiction of five
planetary deities
Cambodia, Angkor Wat, 12th century
Sandstone
Height 44.5 cm, width 119 cm
The Norton Simon Foundation

however, is less well represented in the Simon collection than earlier styles. The three examples illustrated here are a stone lintel depicting five planetary deities (Fig. 16) and two bronzes, one of which portrays the Buddha sheltered by the serpent Muchalinda during a storm (Fig. 17) and the other Vishnu riding Garuda (Fig. 18). All three examples are characteristic of Cambodian sculpture of the Angkor period and reflect peculiarly local versions of Indian concepts.

The planetary deities on the lintel continue the figural type and form encountered in tenth-century Koh Ker sculptures. The mode of representation, especially of the figures seated on their animals as well as their postures, are typical of Cambodian depictions of these gods. Also of note is the conceptual and always frontal delineation of the animals and bird; the Cambodian sculptors seem to have been particularly uncomfortable in representing animals *en face*. However, when it came to

portraying fantastic and mythical creatures such as serpents and garudas, they were extremely deft and imaginative. The charming Garuda carrying his divine master through the air in Figure 18 is a case in point. No less whimsical than the serpents in the architectural section (Fig. 15), or in the Buddha with Muchalinda of Figure 17, the composite creature is just as delightful and animated. Equally uncommon and lively is the diminutive figure of Vishnu, who appears to be dancing as he is transported through the air. Although the iconographic type was introduced from India, no Indian sculptor would have depicted the subject with such levity or gaiety, nor would he have made the Garuda proportionately larger than his divine rider. This reversal of the proportions is often encountered in such capriciously vivacious representations of the theme in Cambodian sculpture. They may well have served as finials of standards and may symbolize the joy

of victory.

The cult of the Buddha with Muchalinda was especially popular in Cambodia, from where it spilled over into neighbouring Thailand. Cultivated by the Khmer kings, the cult had special associations with royalty, which may be one reason why the Buddha is frequently shown crowned and bejewelled as a regal figure rather than as an ascetic. However, this is not to deny the theological significance of the crowned Buddha in later Buddhism. Once again the prevalence of this theme in Thai and Cambodian art reflects a distinct local contribution to Buddhist art. In India the theme is generally depicted in the narrative context of Buddha Sakyamuni's life, but in Cambodia and Thailand it developed into a cult image in its own right.

(Fig. 19) *Makara* and apsara
Vietnam (Ancient Champa), 11th century
Sandstone
Heights 90 cm (*makara*), 71.2 cm (apsara)
The Norton Simon Foundation

Vietnam

Considering that the art of Vietnam is rarely seen on the art market and is represented in very few museum collections in America or Europe, Norton Simon was astute in acquiring three attractive examples (Figs 19 and 20). As in Cambodia, both Hinduism and Buddhism flourished simultaneously in ancient Champa, which was the name of the kingdom in Vietnam. Between the sixth and the tenth centuries, the important cities were Mi Son and Dong Duong in the north. Thereafter the capital was shifted south to Binh Dinh where it survived until the fifteenth century, though ravaged frequently by the Khmers, the Vietnamese from the north, and the Mongols.

The three Vietnamese sculptures are from the second phase of Champa's history. Of these, the pair of *makara* (a mythical aquatic creature) and the dancing celestial female (apsara) in Figure 19 represent a configuration characteristic of the art of Champa. The female, who may represent the river goddess Ganga, would have fitted into the plain rectangular back of the *makara*. The *makara* is also about to swallow a sword-bearing figure wearing a mitre. In Indian art one frequently sees a dwarfish figure attempting to extract pearls or gems

from the *makara*'s mouth; the Cham artists may have altered the concept, as in fact they did the composition and the form of the *makara* itself. The wonderfully exuberant head of this fanciful creature seems to combine the forms of the Cambodian *makara* and the Chinese dragon. As for the goddess, while her form does share the proportions and plasticity of Cambodian sculptures of females, the treatment of the garment, the design of jewellery, her distinctive crown and facial features are all characteristically Cham.

While this sculpture is typical of Cham aesthetics, the charming group represented against a Siva linga (Fig. 20) is more intriguing. Stylistically it is certainly different from the *makara* and its celestial rider. The group represents Siva with his spouse Parvati or Uma and his bull, which is also elevated on the throne. Rather curious is Siva's tall headgear, shaped like a British Grenadier Guard's bearskin hat. Siva is generally depicted with a tall chignon, which is the hairstyle affected by Parvati in this sculpture. It is probable that we are encountering here a posthumous portrait of a ruler identified with Siva. As in Cambodia, the kings of Champa also indulged in their own post-mortem deification. Whatever its origins, the relief is a unique representation of the Uma-Mahesvara theme. Especially striking are the large, open eyes of both deities, as if they were intently watching some astonishing performance. In fact, Parvati seems somewhat frightened as she leans towards her husband, while rather incongruously the disproportionate bull sits unconcerned behind his master like a pet dog.

The selections discussed in these articles include a number of extraordinary sculptures by any aesthetic standard. Whether the sculpture represents a serene Buddha or a dancing Siva, one is overawed by the skill and audacity of the unknown master sculptors of South and Southeast Asia. As Kenneth Clark once observed, the innovations launched by the Greek sculptors in the fifth century BC reached their final expression in the temple sculptures of India and Southeast Asia. The unknown ancient sculptors of these regions were no less creative than twentieth-century masters such as Rodin, Giacometti, Moore or Brancusi with whom they share the

honours in the Norton Simon Museum at Pasadena. It is somewhat ironic and sad that mankind cannot always live in harmony, but fortunately, his aesthetic creations can easily coexist under one roof. The Norton Simon Museum is a particularly pleasant home, where one can at once admire and adore a Botticelli or a Buddha with equal enthusiasm.

Pratapaditya Pal is Senior Curator of Indian and Southeast Asian Art, Los Angeles County Museum of Art.

Suggested further reading

Martin Lerner, 'Treasures of South Asian Sculpture', *Connoisseur*, November, 1976.

Pratapaditya Pal, 'Norton Simon', *American Collectors of Asian Art*, ed. P. Pal, Bombay, 1986.

P. Rawson, *The Art of Southeast Asia*, New York, 1967.

(Fig. 20) Linga with Siva and Uma and bull
Vietnam (Ancient Champa), 11-12th century
Sandstone
Height 62 cm
The Norton Simon Foundation

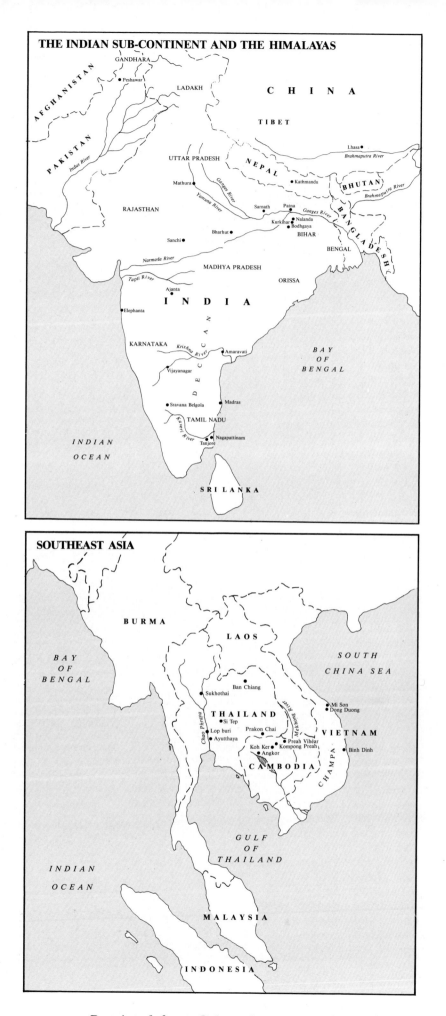

THE INDIAN SUB-CONTINENT AND THE HIMALAYAS

AFGHANISTAN
GANDHARA
• Peshawar
LADAKH
C H I N A
PAKISTAN
T I B E T
Indus River
UTTAR PRADESH
NEPAL
Lhasa •
Brahmaputra River
• Kathmandu
BHUTAN
• Mathura
Ganges River
Brahmaputra River
Yamuna River
BANGLADESH
RAJASTHAN
Sarnath • Patna
Ganges River
Kurkihar• • Nalanda
• Bodhgaya
• Bharhut
BIHAR
Sanchi •
BENGAL
Narmada River
MADHYA PRADESH
ORISSA
Tapti River
Ajanta •
I N D I A
• Elephanta
D
E
C
C
A
N
KARNATAKA
Krishna River
• Amaravati
BAY
OF
BENGAL
Vijayanagar •
• Sravana Belgola
Madras •
INDIAN
OCEAN
Kaveri River
TAMIL NADU
Tanjore• • Nagapattinam

SRI LANKA

SOUTHEAST ASIA

BURMA
LAOS
SOUTH
CHINA SEA
BAY
OF
BENGAL
• Ban Chiang
• Sukhothai
Chao Phraya
THAILAND
• Si Tep
Mekong River
• Mi Son
• Dong Duong
• Lop buri
• Prakon Chai
VIETNAM
• Ayutthaya
Koh Ker• • Kompong Preah
• Preah Vihéar
• Binh Dinh
• Angkor
CAMBODIA
CHAMPA
GULF
OF
THAILAND
INDIAN
OCEAN
MALAYSIA
INDONESIA

Reprinted from **Orientations**, *July 1988*
Printed in Hong Kong